ANNE STOKES
Gothic Oracle

Written by Steven Bright
Artwork by Anne Stokes

Copyright © Anne Stokes 2022 www.annestokes.com
Licensed by www.artaskagency.com

All rights reserved. The illustrations, cover design and contents are protected by copyright. No part of this book may be reproduced in any form without permission in writing from the publisher, except by a reviewer who wishes to quote brief passages in connection with a review written for inclusion in a magazine, newspaper or website.

10 9 8 7 6 5 4 3 2

Made in China

Published by
U.S. GAMES SYSTEMS, INC.
179 Ludlow Street • Stamford, CT 06902 USA
www.usgamesinc.com

Introduction

Imagine a world, if you will, unfamiliar and distant from our own, but close enough for you to relate to; timeless, in fact. Consider a landscape inhabited by dragons and unicorns, filled with lush forests, mountains and rich turbulent seas. It might seem a million miles away but if you take a deep breath and allow your imagination to take you for a ride, it is much closer than you might have thought.

The situations portrayed within the mystical world of this oracle deck are not a million miles away from our own. You might not have a unicorn as a familiar or a dragon to guide you from one place to another but we all still face similar obstacles to the women inhabiting this fantastical terrain. Their desires for joy, trust and true love are no different from our own. The fight for freedom, individuality and justice is the same.

Intuition is a wonderful thing; oracle cards are an effective way of stimulating it while revealing our unconscious feelings and desires. As if by magic, an image drawn randomly can perfectly reflect what's going on in your life and can also provide guidance for what follows.

The oracle has been around for as long as time itself. Our great ancestors would divine messages from the clouds, pools of water and, more recently and with greater popularity, cards. An oracle deck is not only a device for looking into the future but can be a successful tool for reflection, aiding our understanding of current and past events.

Anne Stokes Gothic Oracle is a collection of 48 cards, each with a story to tell. These stories all concern situations and emotions you will recognize from your own experiences. This oracle can help answer questions you might have about your personal and professional life; offering profound wisdom and useful guidance. When used often, the story of your life and those who play a part in it, will mingle effortlessly with those in this deck.

Bonding with Your Oracle Cards

Your oracle deck is a personal tool and is, therefore, a sacred object. You can respect the wisdom it holds within by keeping it safe and clean. Some readers will place the deck in a special box or wrap it in silk. This is an enjoyable part of the bonding process, but it is not absolutely necessary. The box it has come in is a perfectly good container for keeping your cards in order and out of harm's way.

When you open your deck for the first time, leaf your way through the pictures slowly, one by one. Drink in the imagery and consider the various meanings that might apply to each card. You may wish to draw one card a day as you get to know the deck, taking a little time in the evening to jot down your thoughts about how the chosen card's message has been relevant for you. Many card readers begin a journal, ranging from a simple spiral notebook to something more elaborate, where they notate their card draws, readings and impressions.

Working with the Cards

How one reads an oracle is as individual as the reader. Most will agree that there are no rules when it comes to oracle reading but that there are some ways of working that will help the novice and enhance the use of the deck.

A reading can be as basic as asking a question and pulling a card to receive an answer. This is a simple but effective way of gaining wisdom. However, before you shuffle the cards, it is advisable to think carefully about what you wish to find out. Poorly constructed questions will lead to confusing answers, so it is best to be as clear as you can in your query. A question such as "What should I focus on to get the promotion I want?" will garner a more useful response than "Will I get promoted?"

When a card is drawn, give yourself a moment to take in its mood and message. How do the colors make you feel? What are the characters doing? Does the image and title leave you feeling empowered or unsettled? Once you have considered your first reactions with reference to your question, find the prescribed meaning for the card in this guidebook. Does the story add more to your initial response, or does it shine a different light on your dilemma? It is a good idea to make a note of what you have found for future reference, since it may take a little time before the cards begin to mirror what is happening within a situation.

Reading for Others

Once you are more familiar with the *Gothic Oracle*, you will probably want to read for family and friends. This can be a lot of fun but there are a few things worth keeping in mind.

For the cards in this deck to describe real life, there needs to be balance within them. This means that challenging cards often sit beside those that describe the brighter aspects of experiences. For an oracle to be effective, this is natural. Those cards that appear to have less positive meanings might unsettle those who are not familiar with card reading. It is important to make your sitter aware that a reading, however positive and well delivered, can touch on sensitive subjects. It is for this reason that you are advised to build a strong relationship with your cards first, understanding both their light and dark attributes, before you read for someone else. While it can be fun to ask the oracle questions with friends, card reading also comes with responsibility.

It is important to remember that an oracle is a mirror, reflecting our own experiences, feelings and fears back at us. While this can be enlightening and will encourage change, it cannot replace health care professionals. A good reader may see problems related to a person's health in a reading but it is not their job to diagnose or prescribe. If a sitter is experiencing problems with their emotional, mental or physical health, the reader should always guide them toward someone with expertise in that field.

Using Spreads

The placing of cards in specific positions is known as the laying of a spread. A spread can consist of just a few cards or many, depending on your inquiry. Positions add context to a reading and ground the card within a specific timeframe or focus. As an example, "Dance with Death" (a card of risk) would likely relate to something different in a past position than it would if it fell into a placement regarding your future. There are many custom spreads available to try and several have been created just for this guidebook. The reader is invited to create their own too, using their imagination.

Spreads

The Power of Three

The Past, Present, Future spread is one of the most commonly used spreads by practitioners. It offers a glimpse of where you are headed, considerations for the present, and lessons to be learned from the past. When you pull cards randomly and place them into the following positions, ask yourself these questions.

Card 1—Past
What can I learn from my past?
How is the past effecting my present circumstances?
What person or situation from my past is still relevant?

Card 2—Present
What do I need to know about the present?
What present actions will impact my future?
What challenge must I face right now?

Card 3—Future
Where am I headed?
What will be the outcome of my present actions?
Is this a future I'd be happy with or would I be wise to make some changes in the present?

The Dragon's Gift

Place the Dragon Beauty card in the center of your spread, facing upright. Now, shuffle the remaining cards from the deck and place them upright in the positions around it according to the diagram. Each of the surrounding cards will provide insight into a different area of your life and alert you to the beautiful gifts each brings. In all cards (even those that appear to be negative), look for a blessing or warning that can inspire and empower your reading.

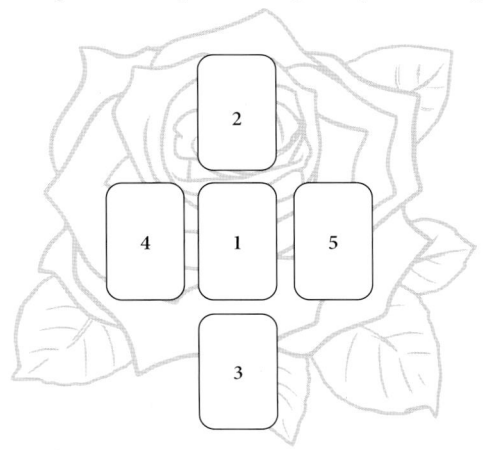

Card 1—Dragon Beauty

Card 2—Element of Air, the mind, ideas, communication

Card 3—Element of Earth, the body, finances, security

Card 4—Element of Water, love, relationships, emotions, feelings

Card 5—Element of Fire, creativity, inspiration, sexuality, drive

The Warrior's Spread

This six-card spread will help you discern what factors are working in your favor to help you take the action for the desired outcome.

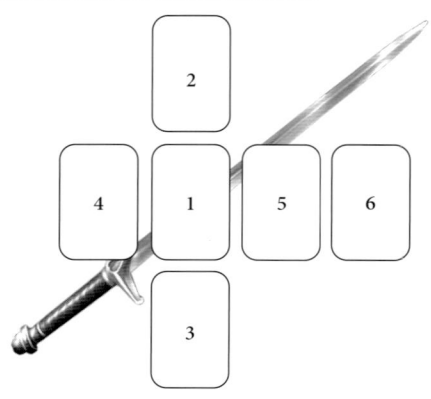

Card 1—You
How are you currently participating in this situation?

Card 2—What you can change
What can you alter for the better?

Card 3—What you cannot change
What is beyond your influence?

Card 4—What to leave in the past
What no longer serves you or this situation?

Card 5—What is hidden
What are you unaware of that could be helpful to know?

Card 6—Advice
What action might help resolve a problem or achieve a desired outcome?

Card
Meanings

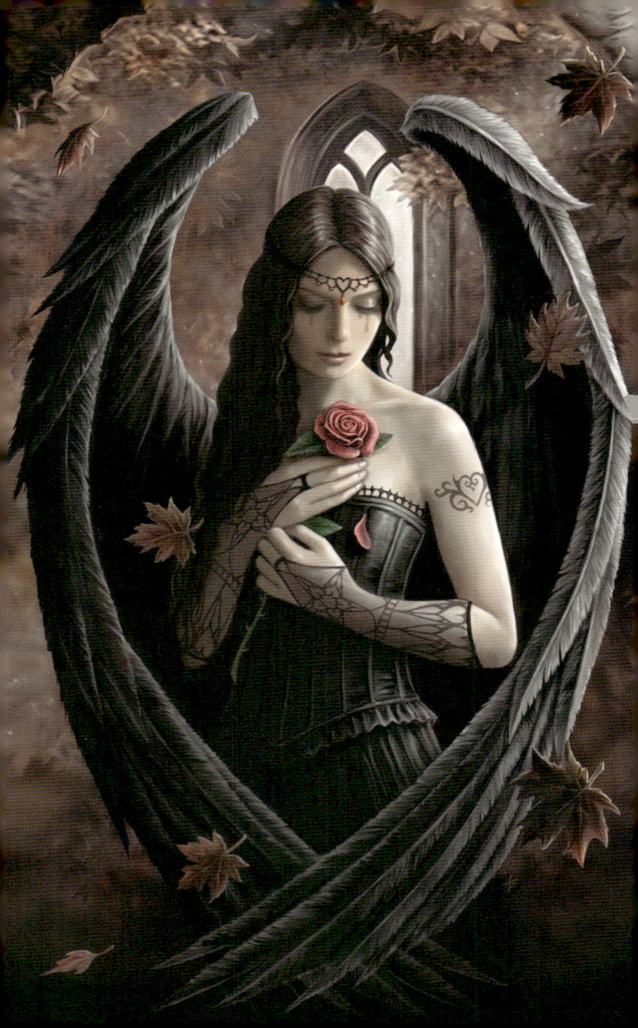

Angel Rose
Perspective

A woman stands with a rose in her hand. Her wings, dark and inky, surround her in the shape of a heart. Amidst an autumn wood, crisp leaves fall around her as she begins to reflect on what she still has, as much as what has been lost.

It is often easier to concentrate on what has departed or disintegrated, such as the dead leaves and the falling petals, rather than focus on those aspects of life that are rich and bursting with potential. There is light behind the woman, suggesting those things that are bright and joyous, yet she remains fixated on the falling leaves of autumn.

A shift of perspective could be needed at this time. While it might be understandable for you to be feeling lackluster or even down, there is always something to be thankful for or to look forward to. Like this woman, just lifting your head up to the light could change your outlook for the better. Though you may have experienced a difficult time, dwelling on a problem or engaging only with those things that have not worked will simply keep you stuck within the darkness.

An act of gratitude is necessary. Even though the difficulties you have faced may have left you emotionally buckled, it is important that you count the blessings that do exist and consider the life lessons that have been gained through recent hardships.

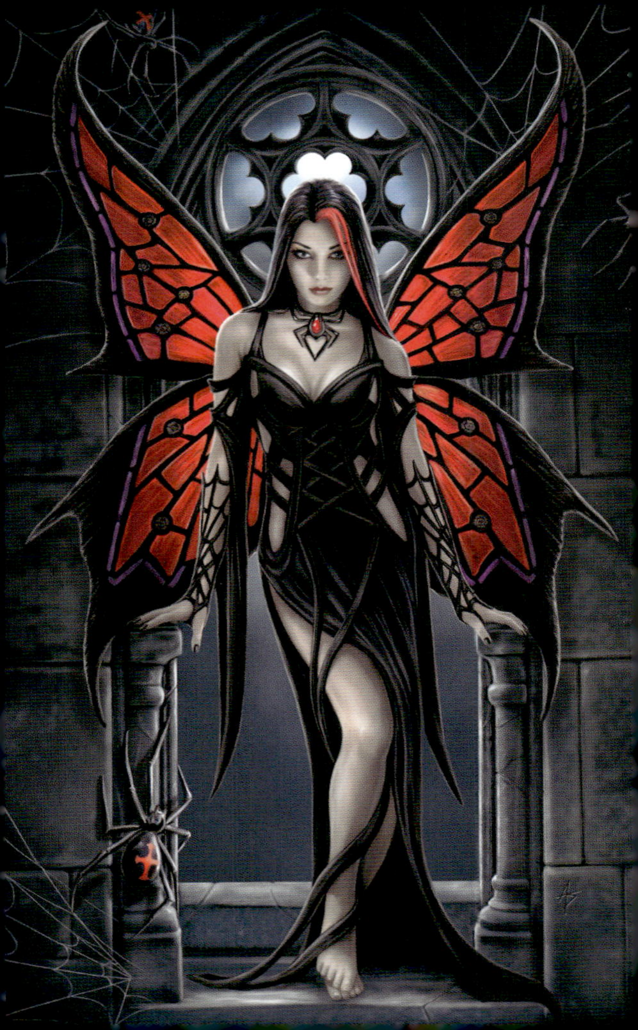

Aracnafaria
Caution

A faery, framed in red feathers, stands cooly in front of a window, the moon gently lighting the back of her head like a soft halo. At first glance, you might think she is here to help or befriend you, but think again. If you look closer, you will see the spiders crawling around their mistress. Look once more and you will notice her necklace, resembling one of her eight-legged minions. The Spider Queen's dress resembles a web in which we may easily become tangled. Her wings are blood red, like the redback spiders that crawl within her lair.

It is only natural for us to be cautious when we are greeted with the unknown. This faery may be beautiful but poison runs through her veins. This is a time, therefore, to find out what you are dealing with before making a decision.

If you have drawn this card, caution is required since rushing into something could result in a bad or even dangerous outcome. If you are considering investing funds, signing contracts or trusting others with something you hold dear, then a little extra research would be worthwhile.

We all need to be cautious at times. Although our modern problems may not be as perilous as facing a venomous spider, they could cause disruption within everyday life. When this card turns up, prevention would certainly make more sense than cure.

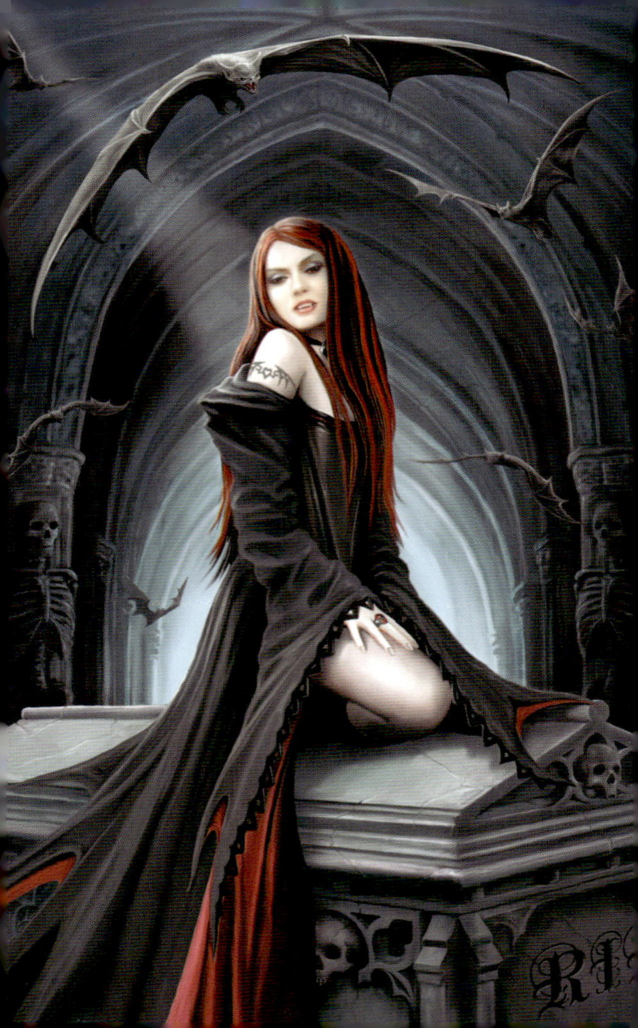

Await the Night
Freedom

A vampire sits upon her coffin. Refreshed from her slumber, she is awake and ready. Bats surround her as moonlight begins to pour into the castle. While vampires cannot exist in sunlight, they are known to wake and hunt under the light of the moon. The night, therefore, is a symbol of freedom for them, since the vampire cannot live amongst the rays of daylight and are confined to their coffins until sundown.

True freedom is living a life that allows for choice without constraints. We might think of freedom as being physical, like the vampire in her coffin during daylight hours. But freedom of thought and expression, especially in being our authentic selves, is a privilege not everyone has the luxury of.

If you have drawn this card, it can represent both the nature of being controlled and the act of releasing yourself from restriction. Now might be the time to fight for your own freedom, whether that means doing what you wish to, saying what is on your mind, or cutting ties with those who wish to hush you or keep you under their control. This card asks that you consider how free you really are within a given situation or relationship. What might you need to say or do to experience true freedom and live an authentic life?

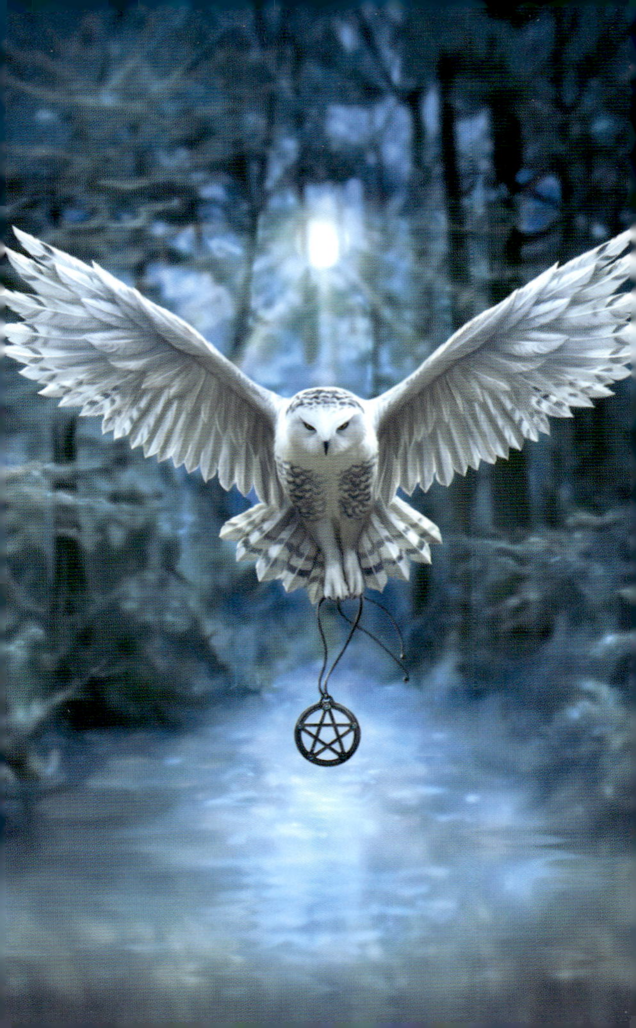

Awaken your Magic
Inspiration and Ideas

An owl in flight heads towards you. The light of the moon illuminates his ivory wings as he prepares to land before you with a pentacle clutched in his talons.

New ideas and inspiration can often feel like the arrival of this bird. They can come from nowhere and take hold of your mind; sometimes they are fleeting, like the owl, disappearing as quickly as they appear. We have all experienced that rush of inspiration, scurrying for a pen and piece of paper to jot down an idea before it disappears.

If you have drawn this card, it is suggesting that you are not only in receipt of a brainwave or creative spark but that now is the ideal time to make use of it. Once we have become awakened by the magic of our imagination, we must consider ways we can manifest this idea in the physical world.

Have you had an idea for something that could change your life or the lives of others? Have you come up with a better way of doing something or found the solution to a problem? Think of practical ways this inspiration can become released from your mind and born into reality.

CARPE ★ DIEM

LETI

MORS

UT VIS ET UMBRA SUMUS

Beyond the Veil
Balance

A veiled woman is poised and still. In her hands she holds a skull, a reminder of inescapable mortality. You will notice the Yin Yang symbol faintly covering this image like a soft film, highlighting the balance between life and death. In Eastern thought, the Yin Yang symbol suggests the two complementary forces that make up life as we know it. The Yin is the feminine principle, suggesting all that is female, darkness, and passivity. The Yang is the male essence, complimenting the Yin with that which is male, light, and active. We all have masculinity and femininity within us. Like the Sun and Moon, these two forces cannot exist without one another.

At the top of the card is the motto *carpe diem*, which means "seize the day," a reminder to make the most of the time we have here on Earth before we pass from this realm to the next. We can embrace this outlook while living a balanced life, experiencing work and play, joy and sacrifice, excitement and calm, in even measures.

If you have drawn this card, it might be that you are feeling the effects of imbalance in your life. If you are socializing too much or working too hard, you may need to realign your priorities to strike a healthy and sustainable balance.

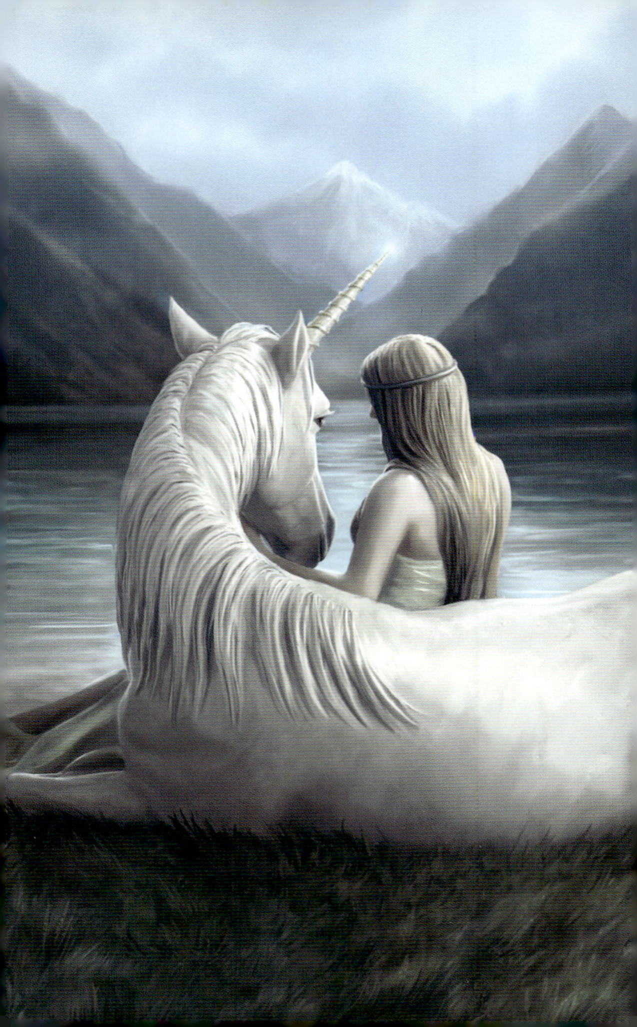

Beyond Words
Friendship

A young maiden and a unicorn sit together in silence; the water before them is cool and still. Though nothing is said, they both know what the other is thinking. Their friendship is beyond words, for they understand one another perfectly.

True friendship is rarer than you might think. A real friend is someone who is willing to join with you in joy but does not disappear when the going gets tough. Have you ever had a friend who is there to both laugh and cry with you?

If you have drawn this card then you are being reminded of an unbreakable bond; one that can be trusted and relied on, but that also brings much satisfaction. The unicorn and maiden are from different worlds, but this does not affect their compatibility. Their connection is based on a soul level, rather than an earthly one.

In a reading, Beyond Words will remind you that someone is there for you. You may think that you know who this person is but think again. In some situations, a supportive or kindly friend may not be the first one that comes to mind. Who has really been your rock through both the good and the bad?

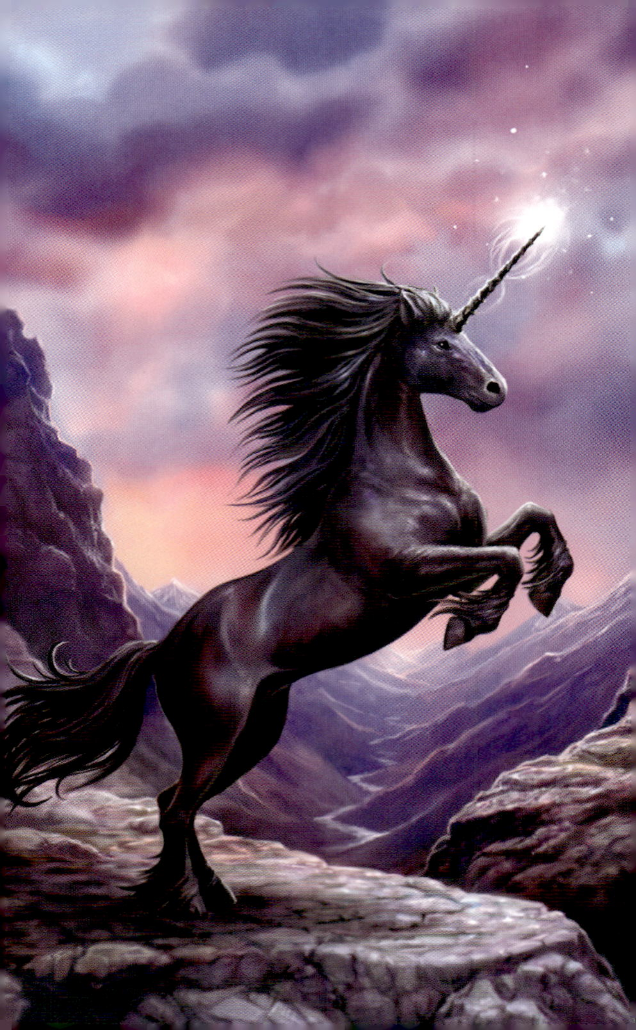

Black Unicorn
Independence

A dynamic unicorn rears up on its hind legs. Majestic and high above the world, he commands respect from all who see him.

Black unicorns are less familiar than white ones but they do have their own place in mythology. Known as a symbol of freedom, their character is not the same as that of their white cousins. With great strength and hunting prowess, the black unicorn is a creature of fierce independence and, sometimes, rebellion.

Occasionally, we need to stand on our own two feet. When this card appears in a reading, it is suggesting that now is not a time to rely on others but to stand confidently in your own beliefs and take charge of your life.

This card is, in many ways, a symbol of choice, since it is in our decisions that we exercise our power and independent thinking. Whether you choose to be self-sufficient and decide to go it alone or make a stand, potentially pushing against the flow, doing so will command respect from others and put you in a league of your own.

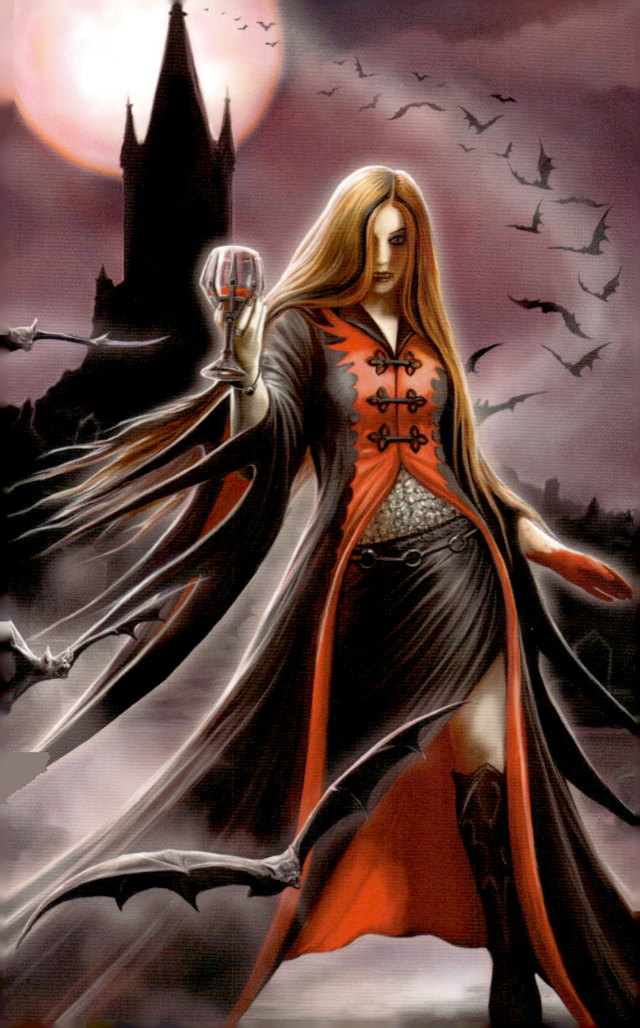

Blood Moon
Opportunity

A vampire stands beneath a blood red moon, the color it takes on when fully eclipsed. She holds out a goblet of life blood, suggesting opportunity and potential. Will you partake in her offering?

When this card arrives in a reading it suggests an opportunity or opening of some kind. In some cases it might suggest a romantic proposition such as being asked on a date, or it can suggest that a potential relationship is in the cards. In a career-based reading, there may be the possibility of a new job or a promotion. Opportunities of all kinds are possible when Blood Moon is in play.

What is important to remember is that an opportunity is just that. While good fortune is contained within the essence of this card, it is only you who can make it happen. Whether you choose to accept the goblet and, therefore, what the symbolic blood can offer you, is up to you. Change and prosperity could be within your grasp if you reach out and take advantage of them.

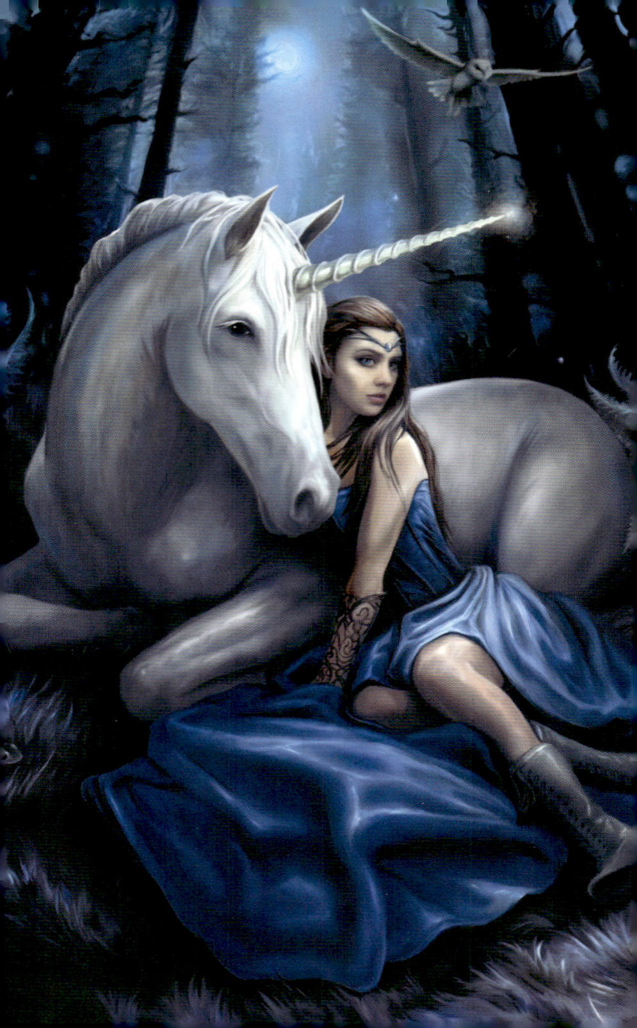

Blue Moon
Luck

Beneath the moon, a girl and her unicorn companion bathe in the blue light. Within the dark forest, wildlife can be seen. In this opportune moment, an owl wings his way through the trees.

A blue moon is considered a rarity, bringing to mind the popular expression 'once in a blue moon.' In actuality, it is the name given to the appearance of a second full moon in a calendar month. On average, a blue moon occurs every two and a half years.

Because of the infrequency of the event, this card is connected to luck and the seemingly impossible becoming possible. When its magnificent glow lights a reading, it suggests that you will become the beneficiary of prosperity. This occurrence, however, may not be expected since the card, like the blue moon, is out of the ordinary.

Luck is on your side. Fortune will favor you and you'll likely be in the right place at the right time! Surprise opportunities and random synchronicities are part of this card's message, whether you find a little extra than you thought in your bank account this month or meet with someone who could positively change your life.

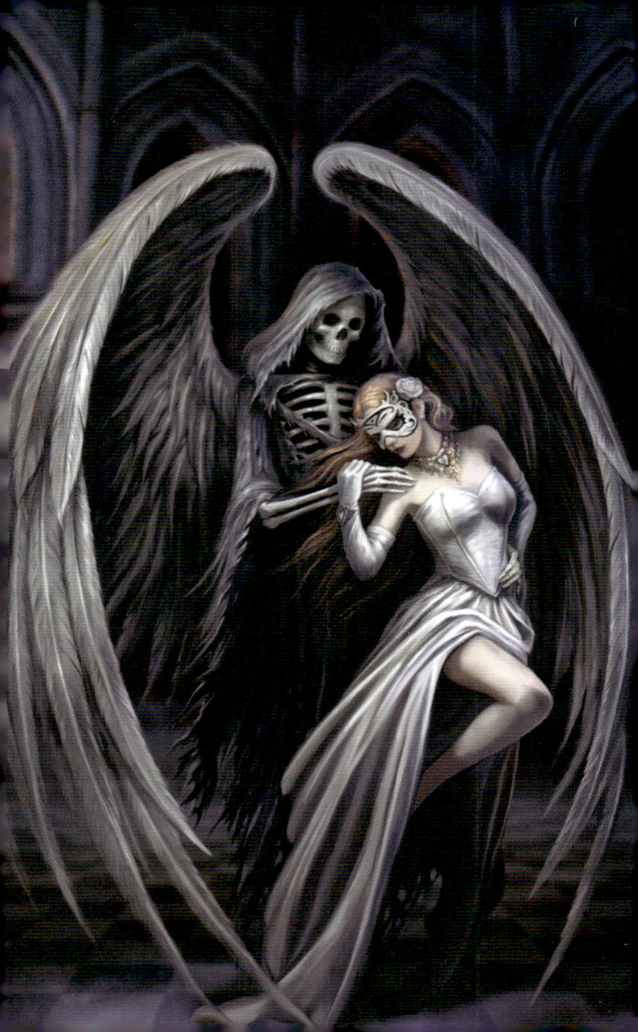

Dance with Death
Risk

A young woman, radiant and full of life, takes a dance step with the Dark Lord himself. With his skeletal fingers tenderly holding her waist and brushing her shoulder, he sensitively looks down at her red hair, adorned with a white flower.

This relationship is reminiscent of the marriage between Hades and Persephone of Greek mythology. Spending part of the year on Earth with her mother, Demeter, Persephone would descend into the underworld with her husband during the time we recognize as winter. While there, all of nature would shrivel and die until she returned to her mother in the spring.

Dance with Death can, at times, arrive as a warning. Are you taking risks that could become hazardous or is a choice you're making precarious or even dangerous? This card urges you to consider what the outcome might be and if you are risking more than you might gain from a certain decision. To dance with death is to potentially make a sacrifice.

When it is at its most favorable, this card could be suggesting that a small risk is worth taking. While you would be advised to not endanger either your health or security, there will be times when taking a chance can pay off or a gamble could reap rewards.

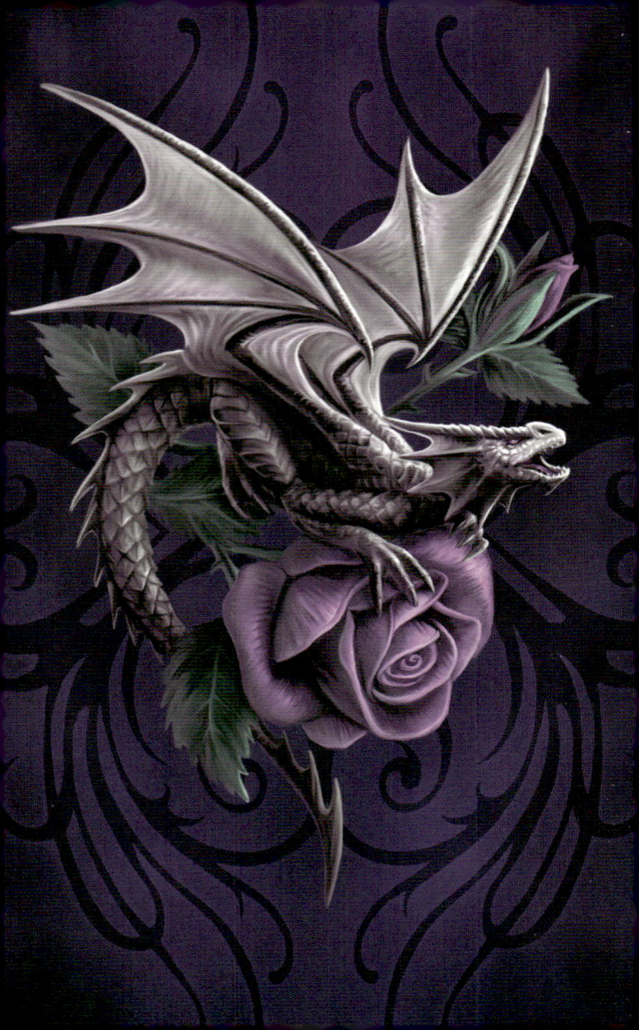

Dragon Beauty
Gifts

A small dragon perches upon a rose, the flower blooming beautifully in both its perfection and natural flaws. The rose, in all its colors, is often presented to loved ones, connoting romantic, caring or kind intentions. With his wings beginning to spread above him, this dragon offers you the rose, a symbol of generosity and beauty.

This is a card connoting a gift, a pleasant surprise or the arrival of something pleasing. It can describe the giving of presents and the generosity of others but its meaning is far wider than impromptu gift giving; Dragon Beauty will, in some situations, concern compliments and can predict praise.

What could be better than being told you are doing a good job or being congratulated for your efforts? In some readings, the card will hint at promotions. If you have drawn this card, then know that the gift of good news is on its way as new opportunities may be headed in your direction. In its simplest of meanings, being reminded of your qualities, admired, or noticed will give you a much needed boost.

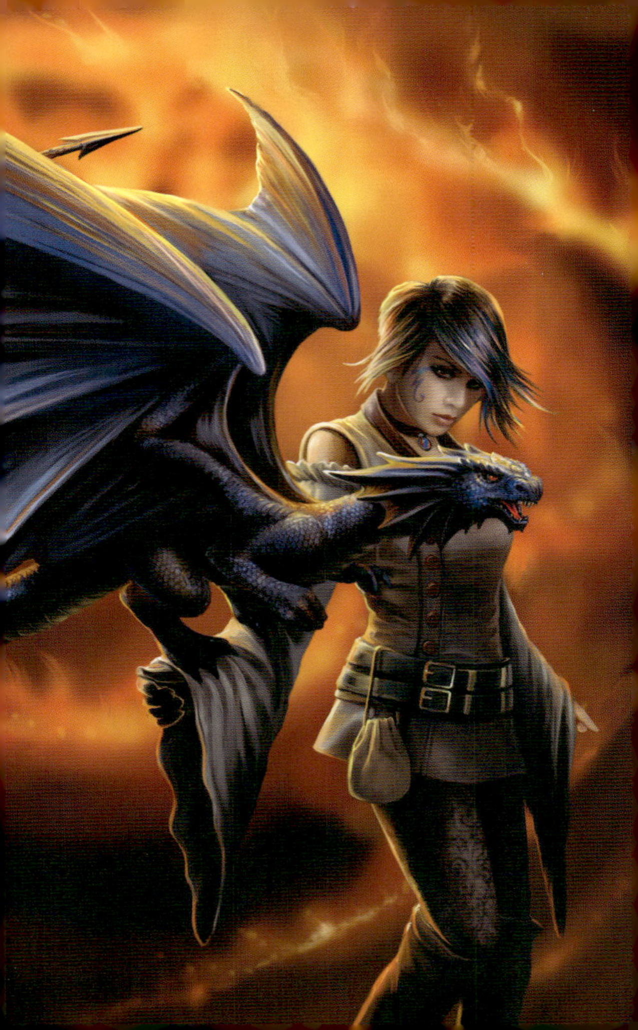

Dragon Trainer
Skills

A young woman focuses on a dragon that has landed on her arm. Fire curls around the two of them, suggesting her confidence and the command she has over her surroundings. The young dragon is eager to learn to fight and to use his skills with great effectiveness.

This is a card of talents, some natural and some learned. The young woman pushes the dragon out and into the air, forcing him to duck and dive between the flames as he attacks his target with accuracy and finesse. With each new flight, the dragon is faster and more precise.

If you have pulled this card, it describes a need for broadening your skills or even, in some cases, the ability to share them. Would you do well to improve your own skill set by embarking on some training or going back to school? Might a little extra practice help you with a pastime or hobby? This card is a symbol of improvement and development of one's expertise, sometimes leading to a promotion at work or gaining some kind of mastery.

In some situations, Dragon Trainer will be asking that you share your own talents. Teaching others something that you have learned or are considered an expert at could be part of this card's message.

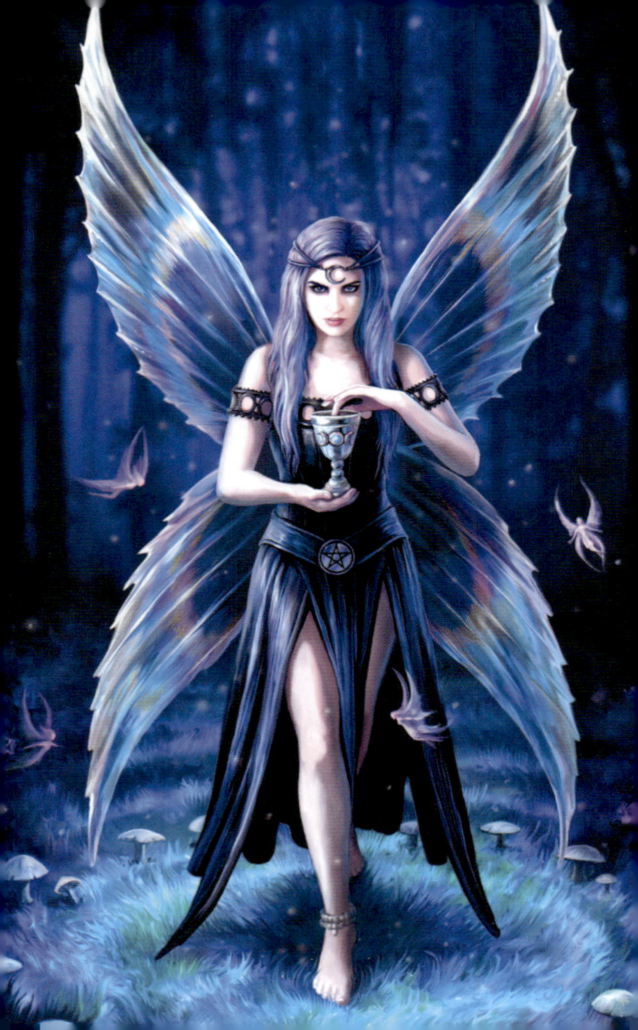

Enchantment
Commitment

A faery walks a path toward us, stopping within a circle of mushrooms. Holding a goblet, she asks if we would like to take a sip of the forest wine.

Faery rings are naturally occurring circles of mushrooms that can be found in the countryside. As the name suggests, they have been long associated with pixies and faeries in many English and Celtic tales. It is said that the rings appear where elves have danced or that a faery village lays underground. Many believe that to stand within a faery ring can bring great enchantment and luck. However, since some advise against this, doing so requires great commitment.

If you have drawn this card, then you are being asked to think about how committed you are to something or someone. Are you all in or are you all out? Commitment comes with responsibility and must not be taken lightly. Are you about to sign a contract, enter into a partnership or are you considering taking a relationship to a new level? If so, make sure that you are aware of what your commitment will entail. While enchantment may very well be the reward, it may be more difficult to step out of the faery ring than it was to step in.

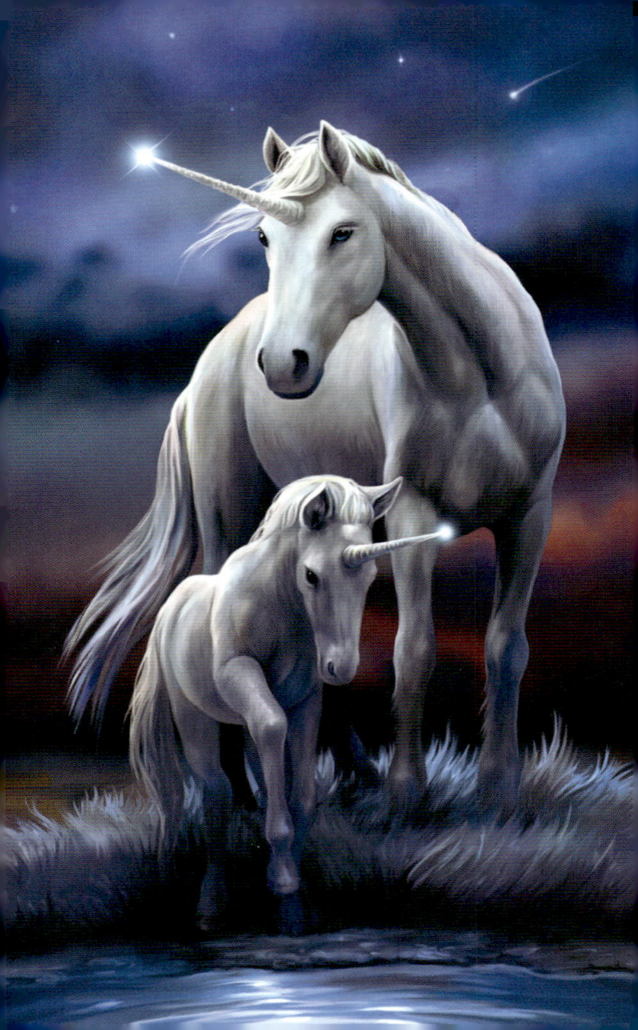

Eternal Bond
Unconditional Love

Two unicorns stand beneath the night sky. The tips of their horns light a pool of water, and the curious foal tests the water with his hoof. Watching the youngster's every move, the mare stands over him protectively. A shooting star can be seen in the distance.

To love unconditionally is to expect nothing in return. The mare in this card wants only for her foal to be healthy, safe and happy. It is natural for most parents to feel this way about a child, but it is not only biological mothers and fathers who experience compassion or offer their love freely in this kind of way. We are all capable of loving without limits.

If you have drawn this card then you might be the recipient of unconditional care, perhaps from a parent, partner or friend. If so, then it will confirm their feelings. However, Eternal Bond will sometimes arrive when relationships are being tested too. It is often important to remember how much you love someone when things are not going as planned, as well as when all is filled with joy. While this card does not suggest staying within a relationship that is making you unhappy, it does suggest that you don't give up at the first sign of trouble. As a sign in your reading, it might simply be advising that you remember why this person is in your life and how much you love them, despite current differences.

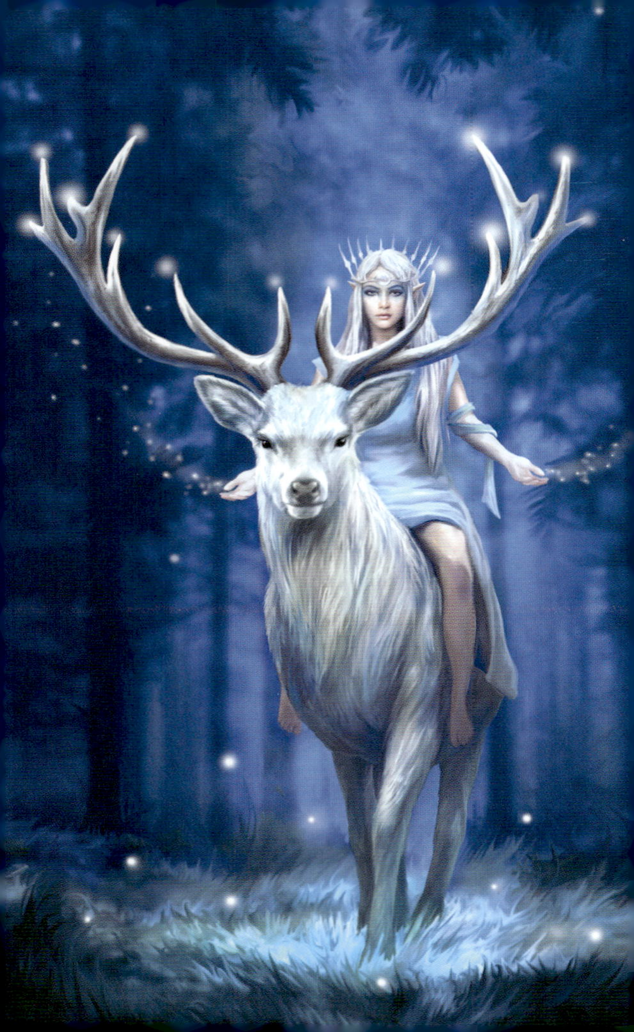

Fantasy Forest
Intuition

A woman rides a grand white stag through the forest, sprinkling the ground with sparkles of light. This majestic animal is often linked to the unseen realms, bringing messages from the otherworld. Here, he is surrounded by nature in all its nighttime glory.

The Fantasy Forest is that place where we can connect with other worlds. When we tap into our intuition or consult with our higher consciousness, this card represents the sphere in which we do it. We all rely on our intuition from time to time. For our ancestors and animal friends, checking in to their gut feelings has made the difference between life and death.

If this card has graced your reading, it's time to consider how you feel. It does not suggest that you ignore logic but, rather, trust in the messages that appear to come from within. Have you ever felt negatively about someone on a first meeting, only to be proven right a few weeks later? Can you remember a time when you were called to do something that defied popular opinion but it worked out better than you'd expected? These are examples of intuition in action.

Some will call it instinct or second sight, even our sixth sense. However you refer to it, you are being asked to lean on yours right now because it has something of relevance to tell you.

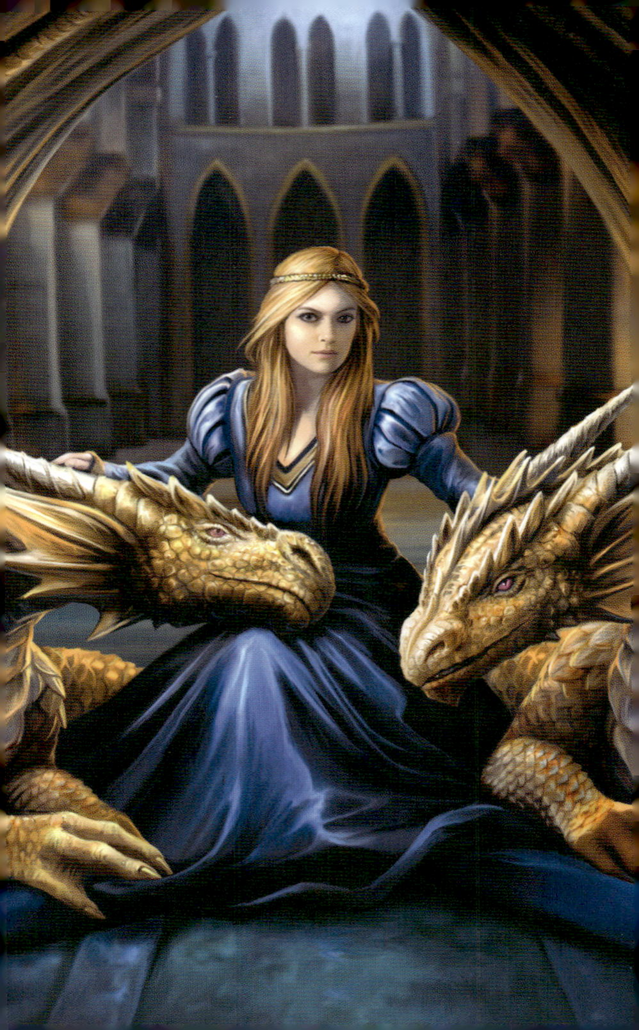

Fierce Loyalty
Defense

Within the walls of a castle, a red-headed woman sits with twin dragons. One rests his head on her lap while his sister stays alert and on guard. Their wings arch above and meet, sheltering the woman beneath. The twins are fiercely loyal and will not let any harm come to her.

This card is a symbol of defense, since it suggests that we safeguard those things we consider valuable. In some situations, this will involve looking out for those who are vulnerable. It can also fall into a reading when there is a need for us to look after ourselves.

If you have drawn this card, it could mean that you or someone you love is under attack. It is important to remember that attacks can take many different forms and preventative measures may need to be put in place beforehand. Are your computer settings and virus protection up to date? Is your home secure? Or might you be divulging your deepest and darkest secrets to those who might not respect them? It may be time to think about how much you share and what the consequences could be.

On a personal level, this card may be asking you to consider your lifestyle. Are you eating healthy and getting enough sleep? When this card arrives for you, think about what you need to safeguard and what will be the most effective way of doing so.

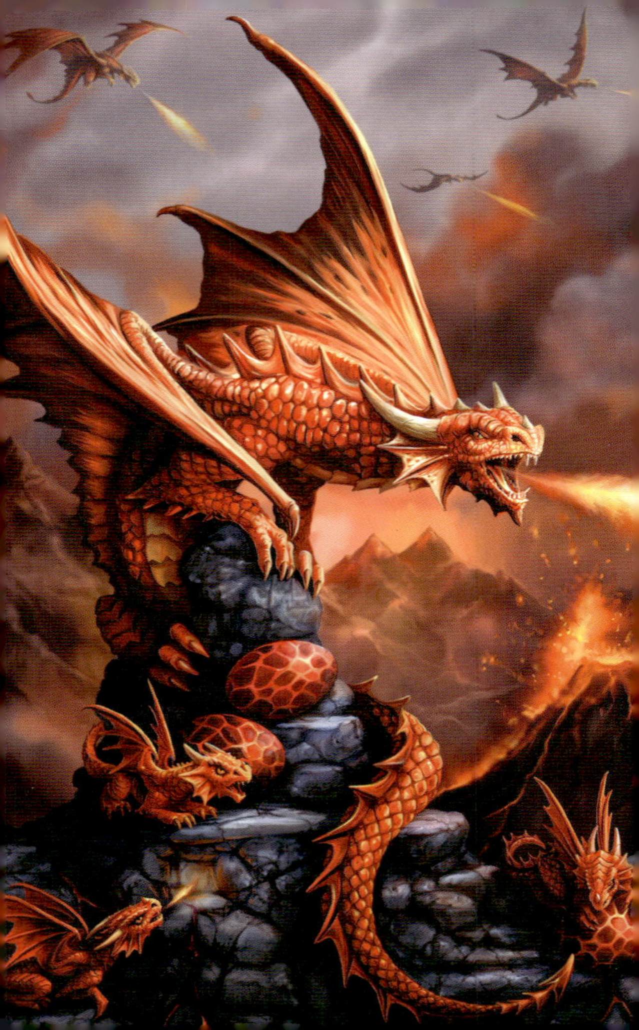

Fire Dragon
A Mother's Love

A dragon arches forward, breathing fire from her gaping mouth with an earth-shaking roar. Her young clamber over the rocks beneath and some of her eggs have yet to hatch. With potential predators in the sky above, she defends her babies as best she can.

When we think of a mother's love, we imagine the gentle rocking of a child in their crib or the tender act of feeding. But when pushed to the limit, a mother's love can be fierce and steadfast. Think of the parent who will do all they can to get their children into the best school or put food on the table. When we love someone or something, there is little we would not sacrifice.

You do not need to be a mother to appreciate this card. Whether it is a child or a new business you are nurturing, it is only natural to do what you can to help it succeed. We dote on our creations and dreams, those close to us and our pets. If you have drawn this card, then you are being reminded that there are no limits when it comes to love.

In a reading, Fire Dragon will arrive to show us what is important and where we must apply care and devotion.

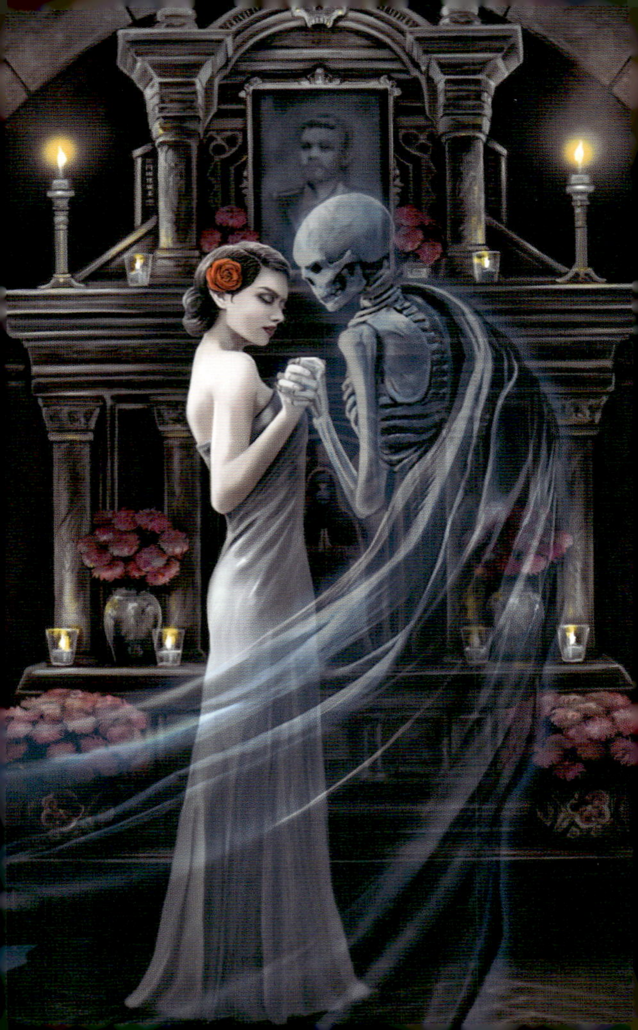

Forever Yours
Love

A beautiful young woman stands before a fireplace with her eyes closed. She joins hands with a ghostly figure, the spirit of her lost love, whose portrait can be seen behind her, decorated by candles and deep magenta flowers.

True love never dies. While this image shows a love that has been lost to the physical world, this card concerns the strong romantic relationships in life that are never-ending: those that are beyond the physical and rooted within the heart.

If you have drawn this card, you are being made aware of a love that is honest and true. The dashing phantom in this card is representative of intimacy and everlasting devotion. In a reading pertaining to emotional relationships, this is a sign of a bond that is steadfast and reliable, but also tender and warm. It would bode well for new relationships and can predict the deepening of a romance and, perhaps, even marriage.

When this card arrives during relationship difficulties, it asks you to consider how deep your love truly is and to be honest in your answer. The love depicted in this card can weather any storm, but it requires the commitment and faith of both partners to do so.

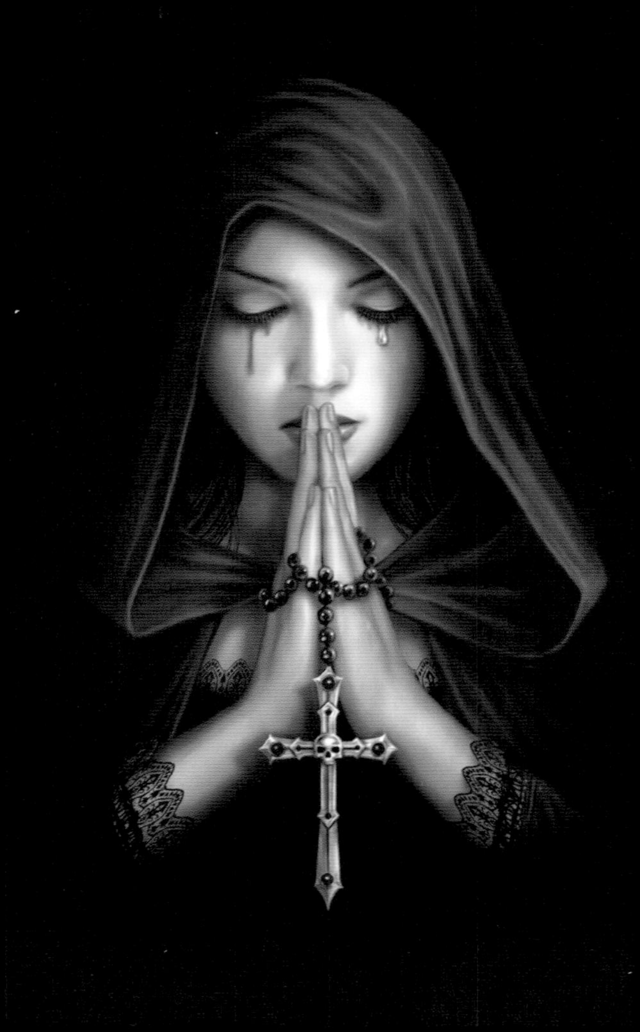

Gothic Prayer
Hope

A woman is cloaked in darkness. Tears gently fall from her eyes, staining her cheeks, revealing her present state of despair. With a rosary wrapped around her fingers, she brings her hands to her mouth in prayer. Despite the shadows that she finds herself beneath, optimism remains.

To receive this message is to remember that there is light on the horizon, however dark and cloudy your personal landscape might feel at this time. You may have been consumed by work, and feel unable to see an end to pressure and demands. Perhaps financial obstacles have weighed heavily on your shoulders or you've become overwhelmed by the problems of others.

We all need aspirations. If you have drawn this card, then you are being advised not to give up hoping that yours will eventually manifest. Gothic Prayer usually arrives at a time when we are feeling lost and unsure of whether to continue. However, for this very reason, it symbolizes the need to carry on and believe in a better time. Whether you have been down on your luck or are simply feeling unmotivated, this card is a beacon of light at the end of a tunnel, providing something for you to look forward to.

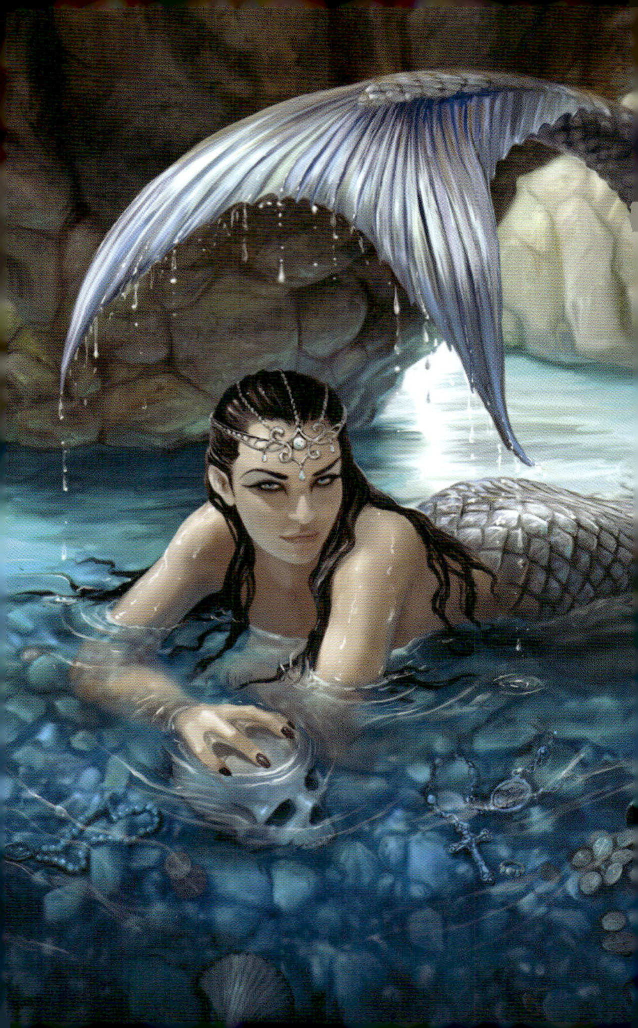

Hidden Depths
Secrets

An alluring mermaid lies inside a watery cave. If you look closely, you see she holds a skull under her hand. Beneath the ripples of the seawater, there are more bones, jewels and money hidden away from view.

Everyone has secrets. Of course, not all of them are scandalous or salacious; some are just those parts we keep deep within that we don't wish to reveal to anyone else. It may be our feelings, personal experiences or, on occasion, things we might be a little embarrassed about.

If this card has turned up in your reading, then it is asking you to consider the value of secrets. Do you have some information that would be best tucked away rather than shared? Now might not be the time to tell others what is on your mind as it could cost you later if not everyone respects your secrets.

In some readings, Hidden Depths suggests that a secret will be revealed by someone else. Something you have been unaware of will soon rise to the surface. While it could be easy to expect the worst, surprise gifts or positive announcements can also become part of this card's message.

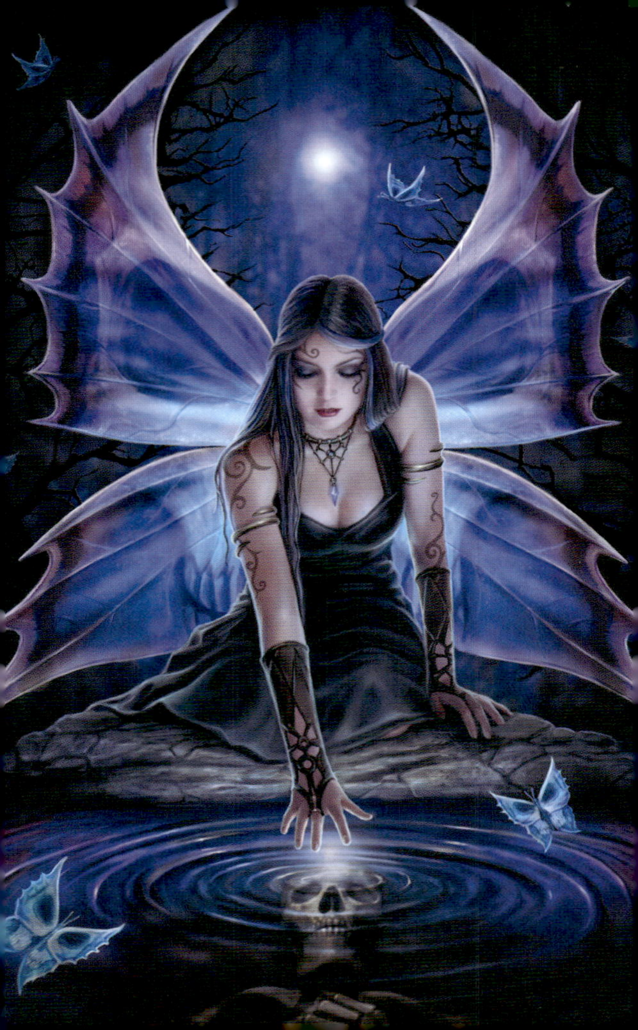

Immortal Flight
Deception

A faery sits beside a pool. Bathed in blue, she reaches out to the water and illuminates a skeleton beneath the surface. Calm and composed, you might think that she has good intentions, but nothing could be further from the truth. The faint image of a skull can be glimpsed in her wings if you look carefully. This faery is deadly. She is a symbol of both the seen and unseen. We can view only what she cares to show us; her true intentions might be hidden. The skull, unrecognizable at first glance, represents what lies beneath.

The motives of someone in your environment could be under question. Is a friend or colleague telling you something quite different from what they truly believe? Does your intuition suggest that you not trust a situation?

If this card occurs into your reading, it could be a warning that deception is near or that someone is hiding something from you. This is a time to do a little research before making any big commitments. When in shadow, Immortal Flight can describe the unfaithful, the dishonest, or those intending to compromise or mislead you.

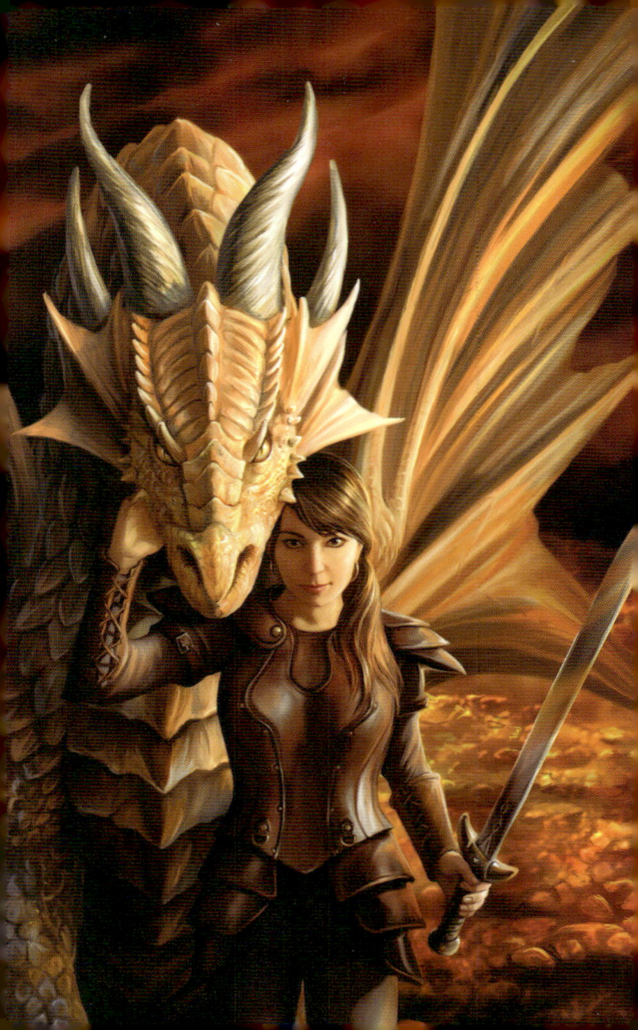

Inner Strength
Courage

A young woman advances with sword in hand. A dragon, adorned with golden scales reminiscent of armor, stands behind her. Their heads connect and she affectionately strokes the beast's chin. At this moment, they are one.

This card is a symbol of strength but not brawn. Is the dragon really there or might we consider that he is simply a representation of what is in the mind and heart of the woman, manifesting her own inner fortitude and tenacity?

If you have pulled this card, then you may need to draw on your own resources of inner strength: your own inner dragon. This is not always easy, especially if it is buried away under doubt and apprehension. We can attempt to find inner strength when we stand up for something we believe in or face up to our fear.

Just receiving this card can be a reminder of the strength that lies within you. If you are feeling less than confident or need to confront something head on, this card suggests that you have the courage to take on far more than you believe you can.

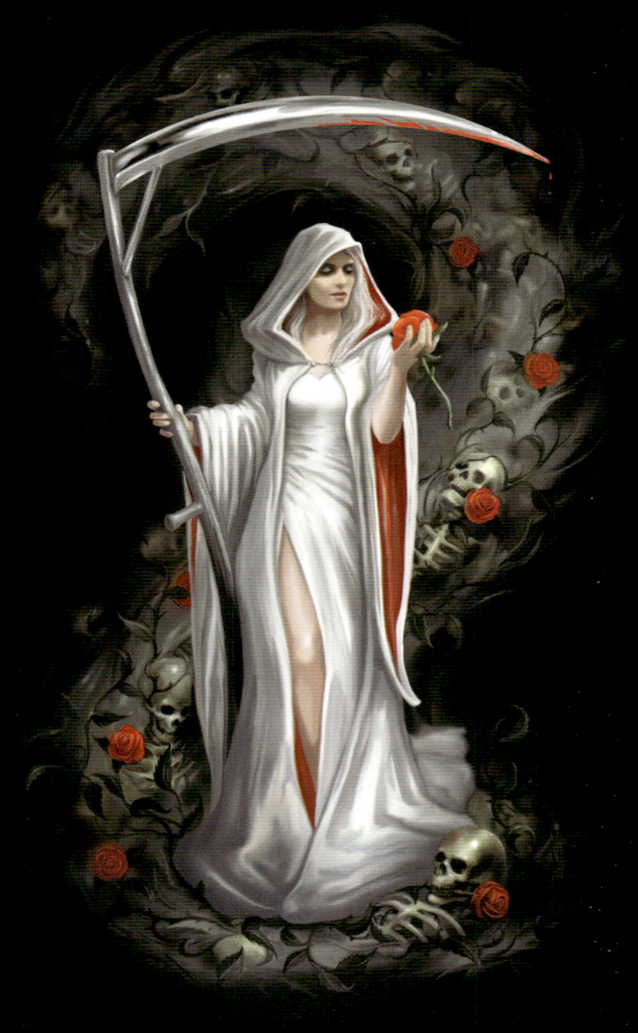

Life Blood
Endings

A mysterious woman, dressed in white, holds a scythe as she contemplates the red rose in her hand. Skulls and skeletons can be seen swirling behind her in the shape of the lemniscate, suggesting that with every ending comes a new beginning.

The reaper is usually dressed in black and tends to be a foreboding character. This one, with her silver hair and youthful appearance, reminds us that not all endings need be tragic or unwelcome. Toxic relationships or periods of hardship have a shelf life too.

If you have drawn this card, then the life blood may be draining from a situation. There will always be times when endings are sad or unexpected, but this card also represents the need to consciously cut away those things or people that are unhealthy or have outstayed their welcome. In this sense, Life Blood can be a positive card, encouraging acute awareness and discernment. Knowing when something is over, however challenging that might be, can be an asset in both your personal and professional life.

An ending may be upon you and knowing that it is either necessary or unavoidable is part of this card's message. The reaper is not a figure to fear but to respect and, in some cases, appreciate.

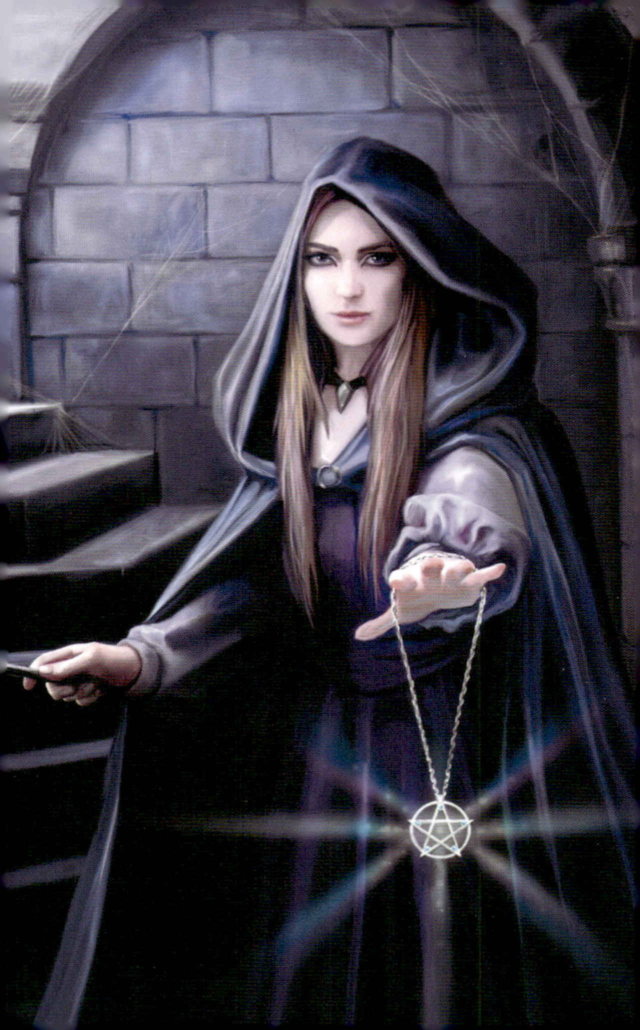

Light the Darkness
Clarity

Holding out her hand, a shrouded figure suspends a necklace before our eyes. The light of the pentacle brightens the dark room, showing every crack within the brickwork and the delicate silvery webs. What we could not see before is now illuminated.

This card cuts through the darkness and helps you to see clearly. During times of worry or fear, it can highlight a positive sign that is headed your way or a snippet of new information that will allow for better understanding of a situation that has been confusing you.

If you have drawn this card, it might be time to still your mind and keep alert. Clarity or understanding could be within your grasp if you only open your eyes and ears. The words of a friend, the lines of a song or a seemingly random message from an unexpected source could provide the answer that you have been looking for.

Clarity shines a light into the darker rooms of existence that are filled with uncertainty. When this card arrives in your readings, know that the situation you asked about will soon become more comprehensible.

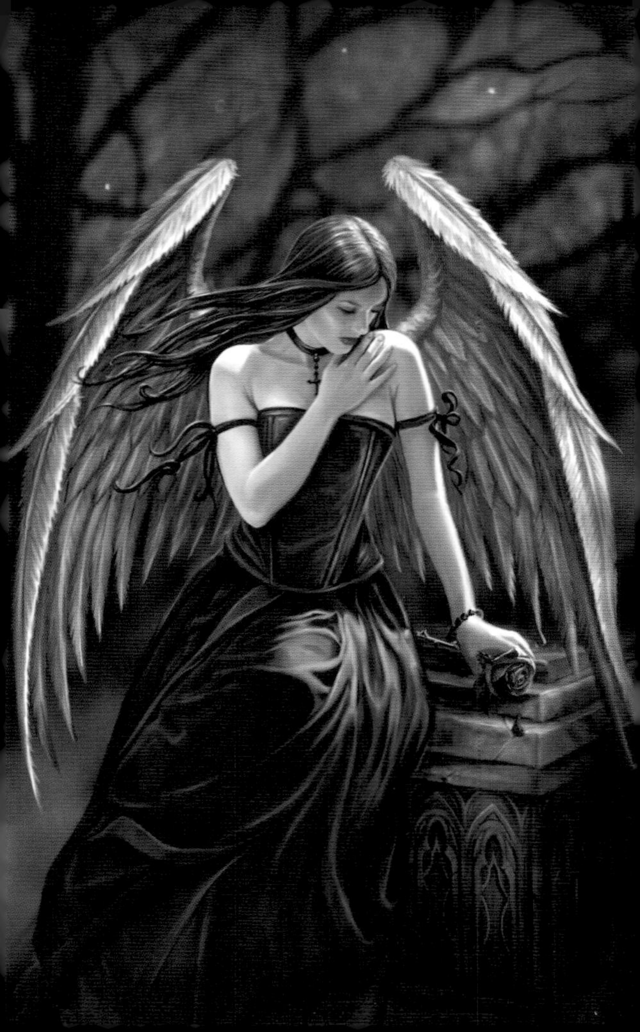

Lost Soul
Loss

An angel sits tentatively on the edge of a tomb. The rose she holds sheds a petal. It floats to the floor like a droplet of blood falling from a fresh wound.

It is only natural that we experience loss over time. Grief and sadness are the effects of losing those people and things we love, and both need time and respect for healing or growth to take place. However, it is important to remember that not all losses will be life-changing or hard-hitting. It is normal for relationships to unravel over time or for situations we once invested a lot of effort into to no longer inspire us.

If you have drawn this card, loss is significant for you right now. You may be feeling sad about the breakdown of a relationship, perhaps, or disappointed about a part of your routine that has ended through no fault of your own. Drawing this card acknowledges these feelings but it also asks you how you intend to move on from them. Although grief is necessary, finding ways to move past your pain is essential too.

What does the rose petal represent for you? What loss are you struggling to accept? Understand that your feelings are valid but staying in disappointment and sorrow for too long might not be healthy or helpful.

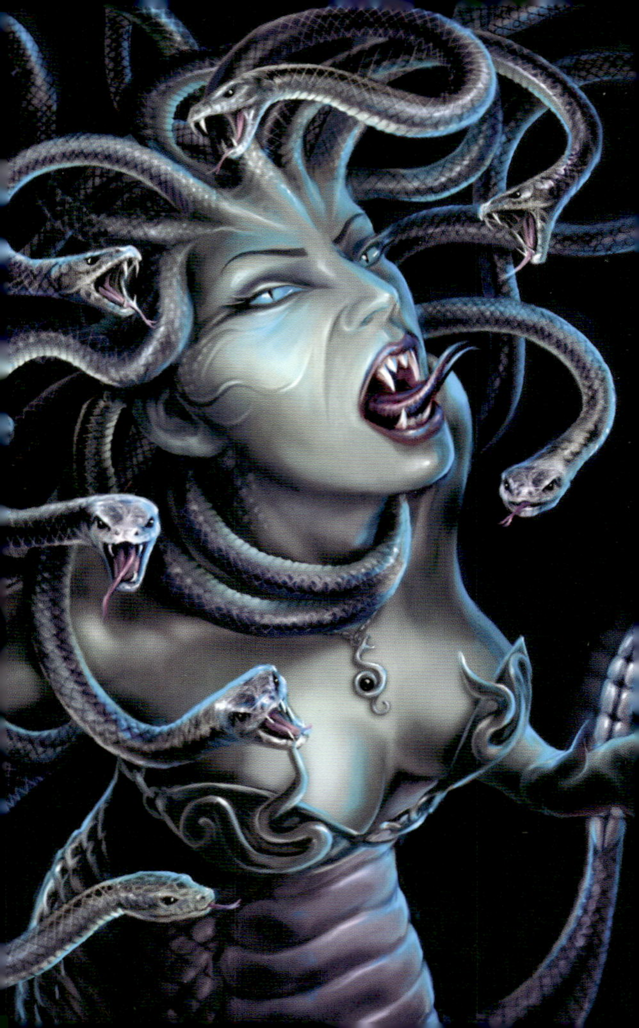

Medusa
Justice

Medusa springs out of the shadows, bearing her fangs and hissing like the snakes that grow from her head. The venomous sting of her tail rattles behind her as she eyes her prey. Just one glance in her direction and her victim will be turned into stone.

There is much said about the horrors of Medusa but we often forget that the woman in the myth was both mortal and beautiful before being transformed into a monster. As the Greek myth goes, Medusa was violated by the sea god Poseidon. Rather than punish Poseidon for this heinous act, furious at the desecration of her temple, Athena chose to chastise Medusa for breaking her vow of celibacy.

In a sense, this card is as much about injustice as justice. It will often arrive when we feel as though we have been treated unfairly. The rage in Medusa's stance suggests a need to right a wrong or invoke fairness of some kind.

If you have drawn this card, it could be time for you to seek justice. You may be motivated by anger but remember to keep as level a head as possible when relaying the facts of a situation. It is time for you to give your side of the story. As a general card, Medusa is a good omen, especially when connected to legal situations or times when the truth needs to be confronted.

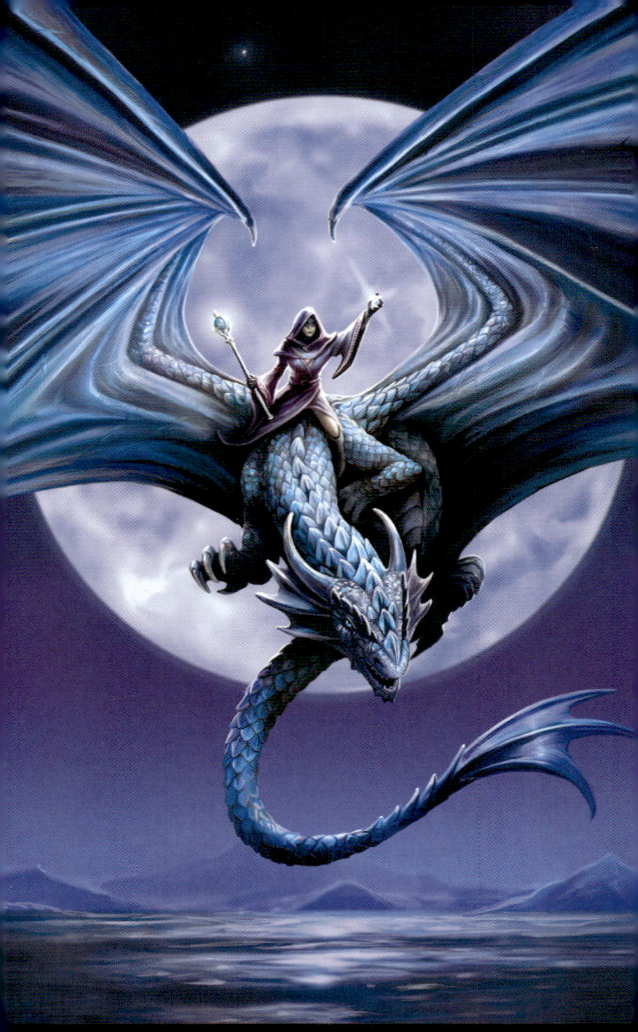

Moonstone
Healing

A dragon and her passenger descend from the moon. In her mistress's left hand is a glowing moonstone, in her right, a staff.

Moonstone is a creamy colored crystal, tinted with yellow. Known for its feminine qualities, such as intuition, passivity and the enhancing of psychic abilities, it is also associated with healing.

If this card has glided into your reading, then healing may be either available or necessary. We do not always realize when it is needed but this card could be advising you to think about those areas of your life that are causing pain. This distress could be recent or may concern older experiences that have been avoided thus far.

Making the decision to heal is not one we should take lightly; it is something that requires participation, courage and commitment. While some of us might enlist the help of a professional (such as a counselor or doctor), just becoming aware of our wounds and how they still affect us can be the first step towards recovery and healing. What is still causing you distress? How might you begin to release yourself from these memories or emotions in a healthy way?

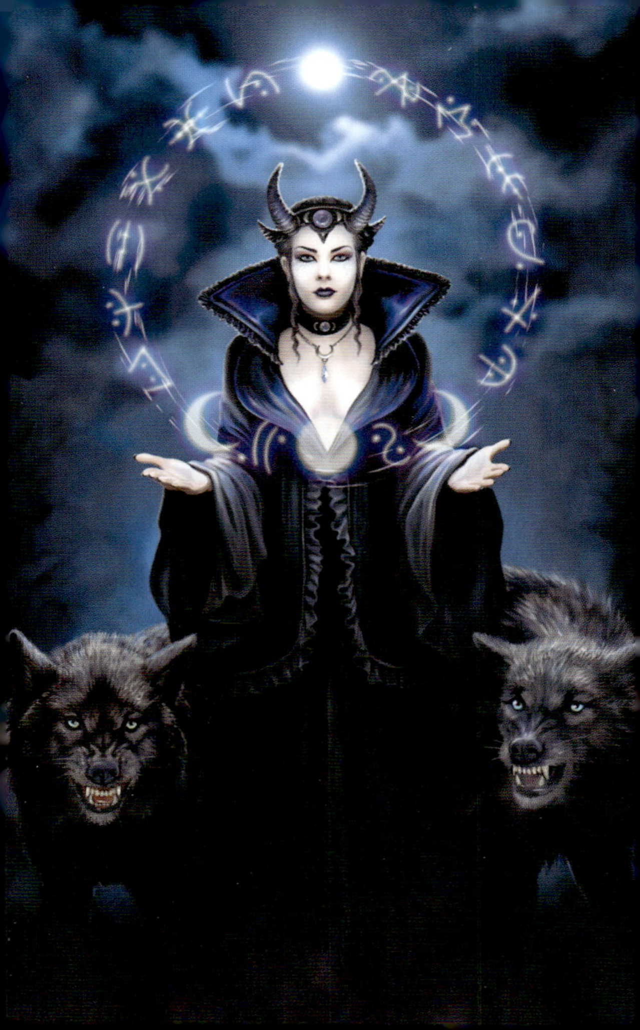

Moon Witch
Manifestation

A dark goddess, dressed in an ebony robe and with a horned headdress, stands between a pair of fierce wolves. Under a cloudy night sky, she summons glowing symbols that relate to the intense blue moon behind her.

Manifestation takes time and will not happen overnight. For you to achieve something, you will need to believe that it can happen and there will be steps that need to be taken. This card does not suggest that we can simply conjure up the things we wish for in seconds. Rather, it encourages us to believe that they can be accomplished through hard work and determination.

If you have drawn this card, then you are being called to manifest something that is important to you. The power of belief can turn a dream into a reality, but it will only do half of the job. For example, if you would like to be published, visualizing your name on the spine of a book is a great way of letting the Universe know your intentions. However, your manuscript will not write itself. Let this card inspire you to actively bring your dreams into existence!

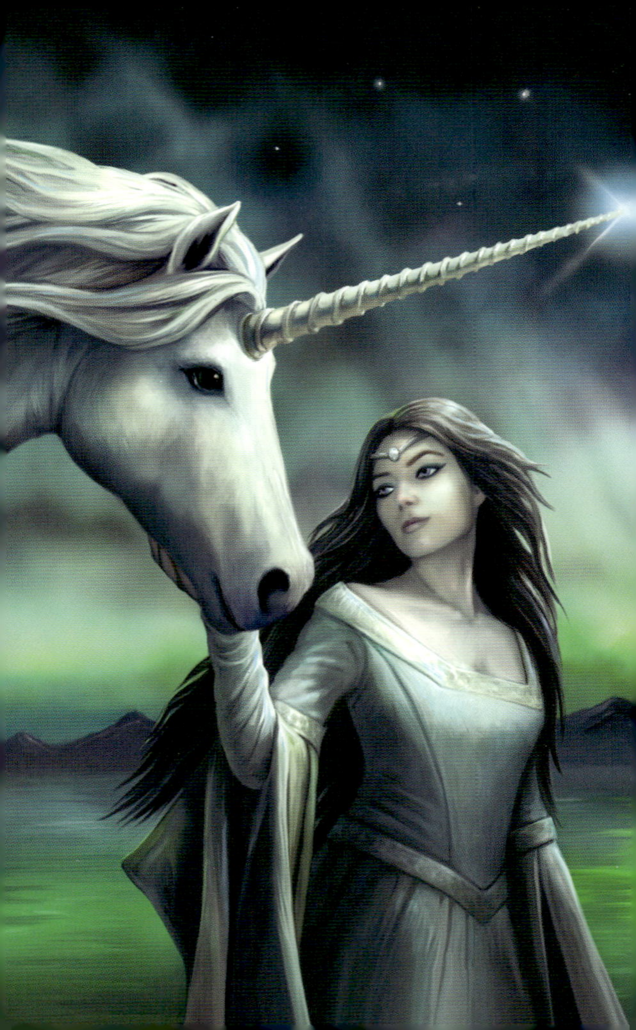

North Star
Acceptance

A unicorn appears to smile as a young woman tenderly strokes his chin. His single horn points towards a bright star in the sky: this is the North Star, also known as Polaris. This star is one of the most well-known astral bodies. It remains in the same spot above the northern horizon all year, while the other stars circle around it.

The North Star is a fixed symbol and doesn't change. It doesn't rise or set. With this in mind, the card represents those things that refuse to budge or which we cannot control. Despite being the architects of our lives, there will always be some things that cannot be altered.

If you have drawn this card, then you are being reminded that not everything can be fixed or changed to suit. We can't control the weather on our wedding day, for example, or change someone's mind once it is made up.

In a reading, you may be advised not to pursue something as it is clearly not working. While you may be in a position to move some mountains, there will always be some challenges that cannot be overcome. Accepting that not every hurdle can be jumped is a sign of maturity and could save you a lot of disappointment.

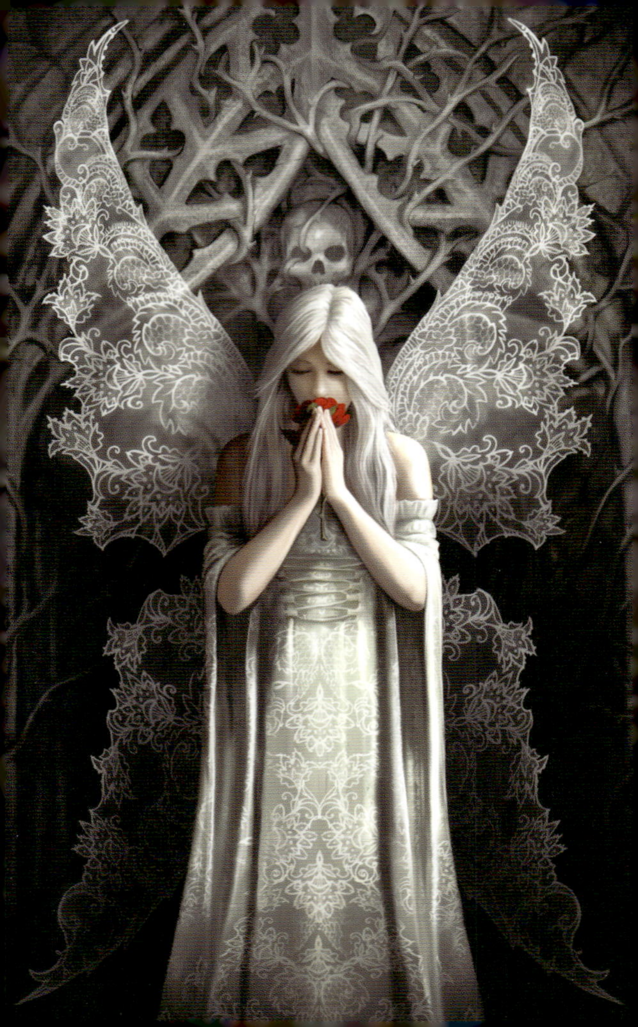

Only Love Remains
Memories

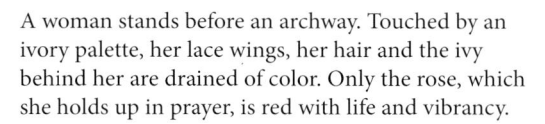

A woman stands before an archway. Touched by an ivory palette, her lace wings, her hair and the ivy behind her are drained of color. Only the rose, which she holds up in prayer, is red with life and vibrancy.

The woman in this card is at one with her memories. She breathes them in and they give her life. Anybody who has lost a loved one or feels that their best times have passed will be able to relate to this. It might feel like only their memories, and love, remain.

If you have drawn this card, it means that the past is of some significance to your question. While you may feel as though your life is now colorless without something or someone you held dear, this may not be wholly true. This card is a reminder of the good times and a chance to reminisce, but also reminds us of the danger that living in the past can bring. There is always more to achieve and enjoy.

As a card of times gone by, Only Love Remains will simply alert you to the past in some readings. A solution could be found in a previous life lesson or, in some instances, someone from your past could make a reappearance.

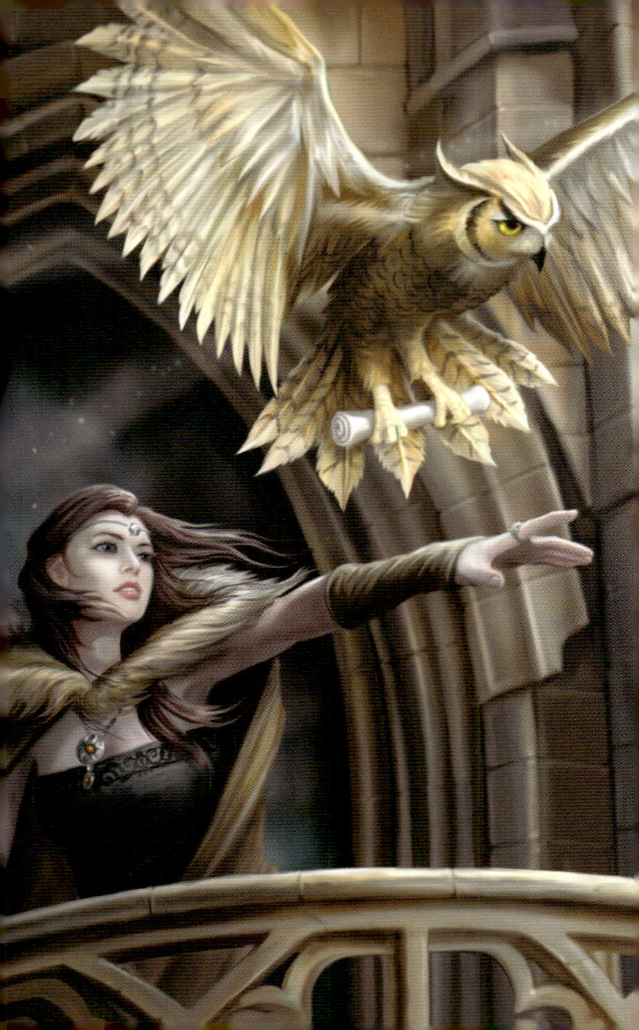

Owl Messenger
Communications

A young woman casts an owl from her balcony. Holding a scroll between its claws, the bird flies into the sky with great speed and its eyes firmly set on its destination.

In our modern age, we receive many messages throughout our day. We no longer rely on just the mail carrier to deliver letters and documents since we now have an array of electronic means for sending and receiving information.

If you have drawn this card, it would seem that a message is headed in your direction. Is this information or confirmation you have been waiting on or will it be a complete surprise? As well as personal greetings, letters and general correspondence, the card also suggests contracts or much-awaited test results.

Although Owl Messenger can predict mail arriving on your doorstep, it can also encourage you to put pen to paper, so to speak. Have you got forms that need filling out and sending or might a loved one appreciate a call or some kind of contact? A message could make their day.

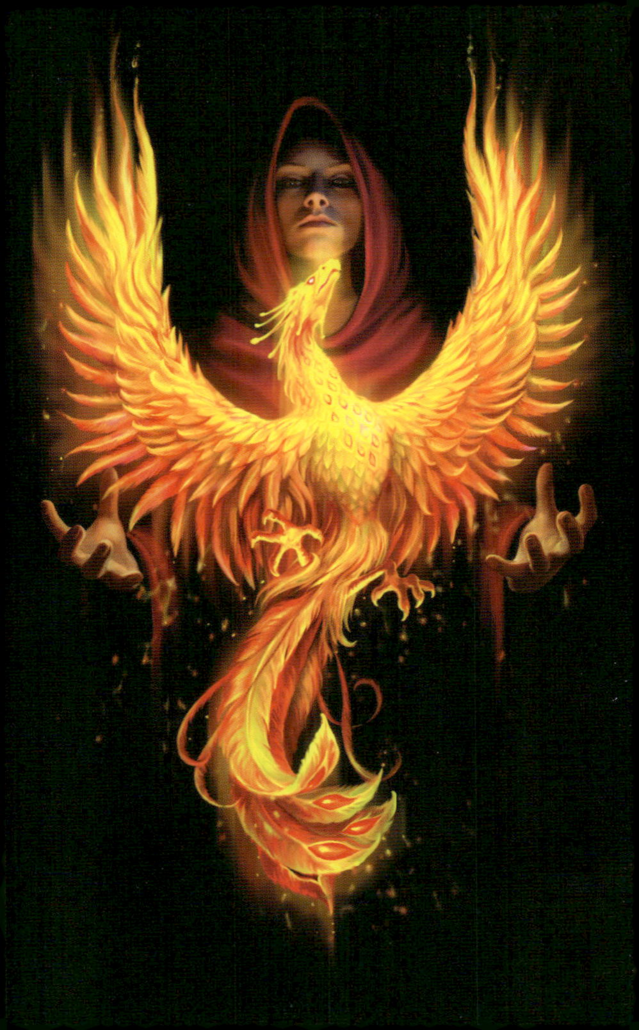

Phoenix Rising
New Beginnings

A hooded woman stands within the darkness, concentrating. With her hands cupped upwards and her fingers stretched, she summons the phoenix from the flames. A proud animal rises before her, suggesting a new and brilliant start.

Every good story has a beginning but you will find that most, like life, are made up of many endings and starts. One cannot exist without the other. For a journey to begin, the phoenix must leave something behind her.

If you have drawn this card, you are embarking on a new journey. This could be a physical endeavor, such as a trip over land, sea or by air, but it might also describe the start of a college course, a pregnancy, a house move or a new relationship. In some cases, it will indicate a new start that inevitably grows from the ashes of difficulty or a challenging situation. If you have not yet begun a significant new stage in your life, then this card could be suggesting you are ready to.

Phoenix Rising is an exciting card to receive. As well as a call to action, it is a beacon of promise for those who are currently experiencing a dark night of the soul.

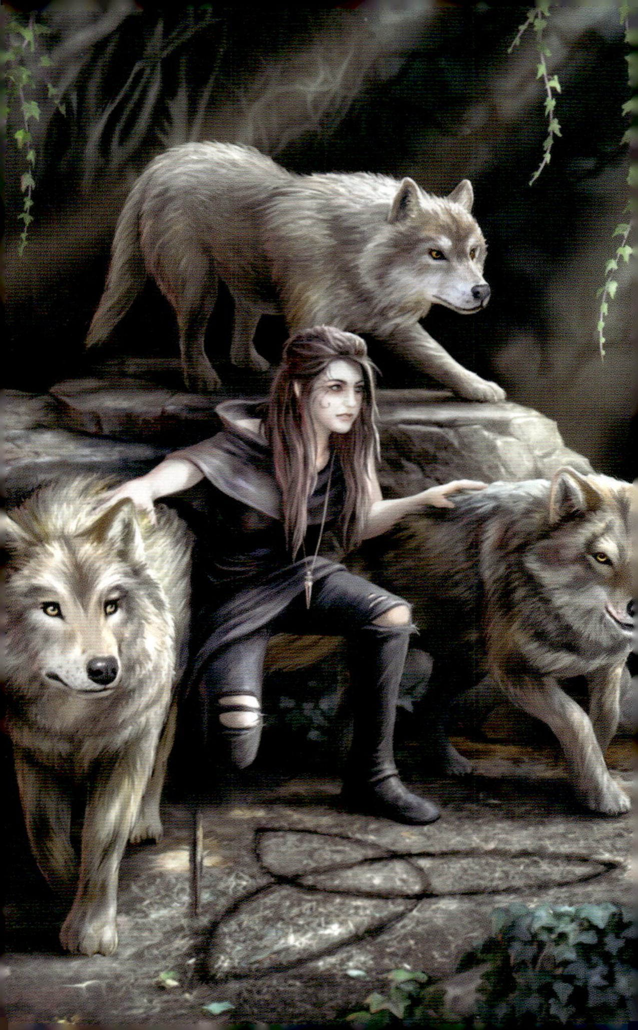

Power of Three
Cooperation

Three wolves take their places around a young woman. All four of them are poised and ready to jump into action. The symbol of the triquetra has been etched into the ground before them, meaning the power of three.

While the power of three could refer to the help of the three wolves—the woman's familiars—it signifies any kind of cooperation or teamwork. Each member of the group has their part to play. Like the cogs in a machine, things will work less effectively if one of them is missing.

If you have drawn this card, it means that the team is of great importance. You may be able to solve a problem or take on a new responsibility alone, but do you have to? Sometimes, jobs can be more enjoyable when we share the experience with others.

Are you carrying your workload and doing your part? Are others shouldering responsibilities that you should be dealing with or is it someone else who has become lax? The Power of Three reminds you of the strength of the group and not the individual. It is often when we all join together that great successes happen.

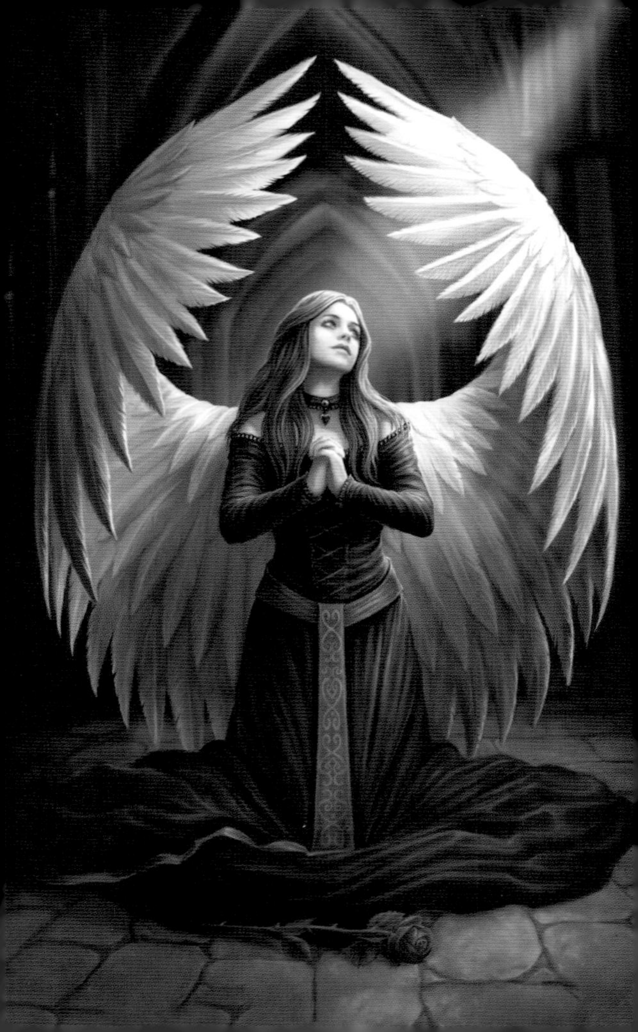

Prayer for the Fallen
Forgiveness

An angel kneels in prayer. She clasps her hands together, offering a beautiful rose that she lays before her. Her prayer is for the fallen; not only for the dead but for those who have done us wrong or caused grief or sorrow.

We are often reminded of the importance of forgiving though not forgetting. It is likely that most of us have been wronged or hurt over time, each of us carrying the wounds within our heart or current circumstances. While we will never forget the pain that has been inflicted on us, the act of forgiving releases us from the emotions of anger and bitterness that we have incurred. To forgive someone for a selfish or unreasonable act may not be easy but holding on to suffering and resentment can be detrimental to our mental, emotional and physical health. It is important to remember that forgiveness is not necessarily something we do for others but for our own good.

If you have drawn this card, then maybe it is time to forgive someone. This does not mean letting them off of the hook. In some cases, it can strengthen relationships by encouraging boundaries if the relationship is to continue. Experience can become a good teacher. Forgiveness is, therefore, the gift we give to our self, releasing us from resentment and allowing us to move on.

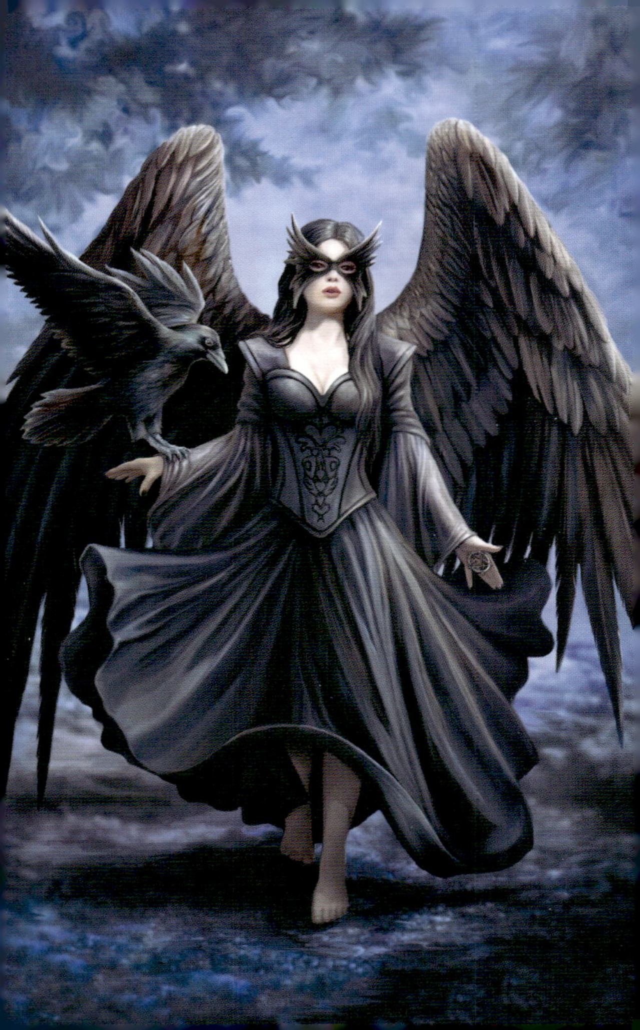

Raven
Shapeshifting

With a raven on her wrist, this young woman with her jet-black hair and midnight blue dress, seems to be in the process of transforming. With wings sprouting from her back and feathers spreading across her cheeks like a mask, she begins to take on the identity of her familiar.

Shapeshifting is the ability to physically transform and can be found in mythology and folklore. From the Greek gods, such as Zeus (who changed his identity to a swan to seduce Leda), to the Celtic tales of Ceridwen and Gwion (Gwion escaped Ceridwen's clutches by transforming into a hare), there are many fantastical stories of gods and goddesses altering their appearance.

There are times when we all shapeshift in daily life, such as when we put on a brave face or mask disappointment. We might do this to protect our own emotions or other people's but there are times when imitation can be of even greater use.

If you have drawn this card, it might be time to shapeshift. If you are hoping to secure that high-profile job, then you might need to dress or sound the part. If you want to invite love and kindness into your life, then displaying those qualities could help compassion find you. The woman in this card is manifesting qualities inherent within her that will assist her journey. How can you embrace yours?

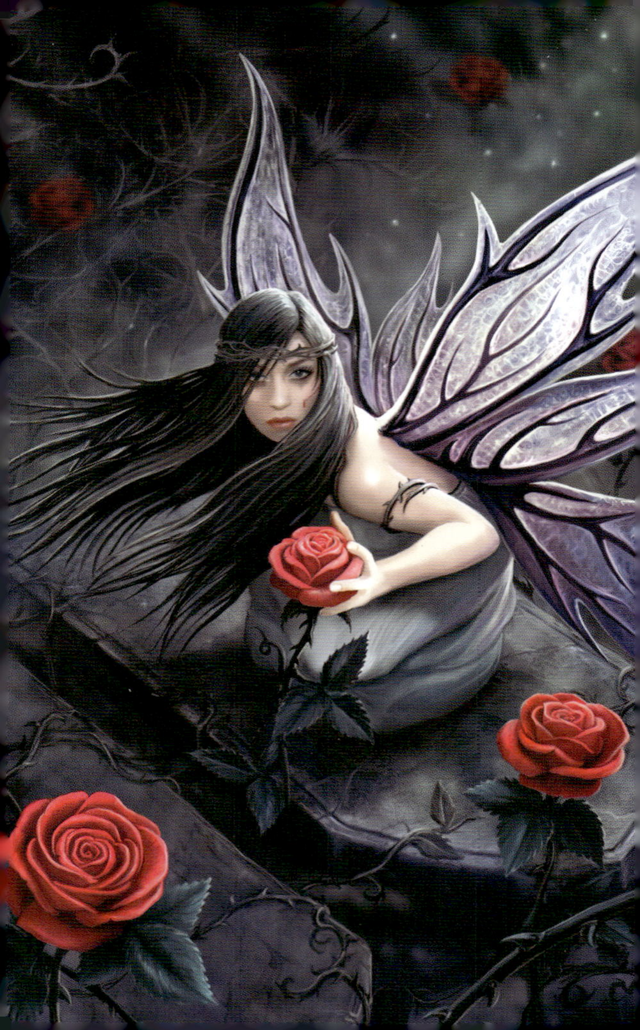

Rose Faery
Pain

A windswept faery lands on a tomb where beautiful blood-red roses grow. They are enticing but one must remember that every rose has its thorns.

Love, in its many forms, is something most of us desire; whether it is the care and attention of a lover or the warmth of a friend, parent or child that you yearn for. Like the red rose, a symbol of romantic love, it can be beautiful as it unfolds from a first delicate meeting to a committed relationship in bloom. However, to be open to love is to be vulnerable to pain. One cannot exist without the other, like the crimson flower decorated by her thorns.

If you have drawn this card, you may have been scratched by the sharp edges of love. To give your heart, romantically or otherwise, may have left you unguarded and prey to the dishonesty of others or unkindness of circumstance. Unfortunately, love and pain are intimate sisters, unable to be separated.

You may be feeling hurt, in grief or are resting beneath a cloud of personal tragedy. The only way of moving through this is to accept that life, and love, is a mix of light and darkness, if healing is to become your next step. Take time to grieve and recover but remember that you are strong enough to overcome the trials you are facing.

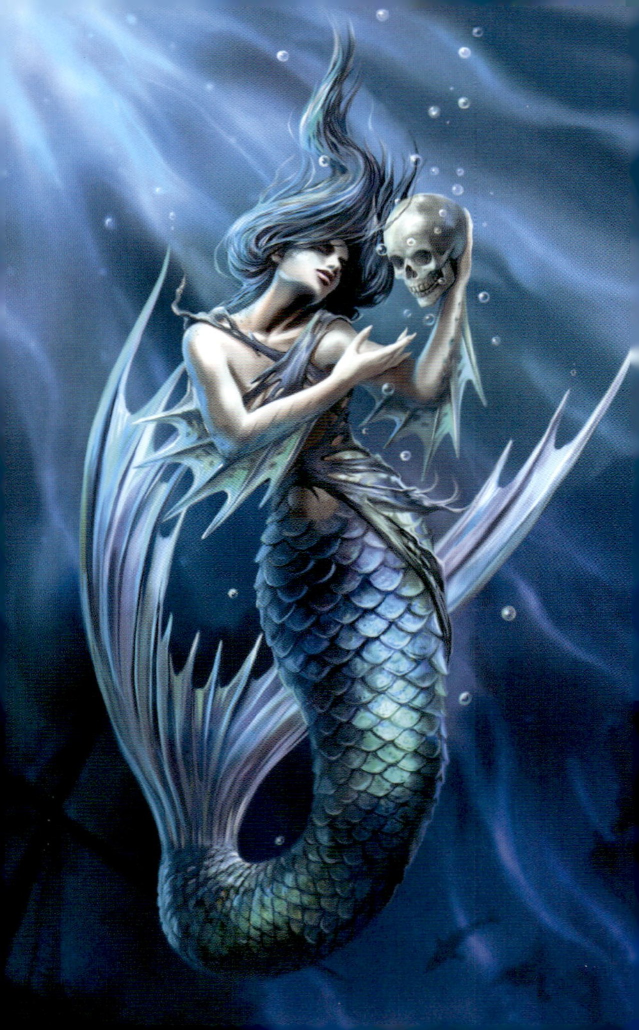

Sailor's Ruin
Temptation

With the light draining from above, a mermaid descends into the shadowy depths of the sea. The faint silhouettes of sharks, representing danger, and a shipwreck can be glimpsed in the darkness. She holds a skull in her hand; most likely a sailor she has lured to his death with her beauty.

We can all relate to temptation in its many guises. If it is not physical beauty that seduces us beyond our limitations, then it can be wrapped up in many other attractive packages such as food, alcohol, laziness, overspending or a bad choice of partner. The sailor's ruin is in his lack of resistance.

If you have drawn this card, you may have already succumbed to temptation or may be on the brink of doing so. Sometimes, the people and things we know are not good for us become the most attractive and persistent options. Sailor's Ruin reminds you that most desires, such as the odd treat or letting your hair down, can actually be beneficial in moderation. However, too much of a good thing can become detrimental. What is tempting you at this time and what might be the cost of giving into your urges?

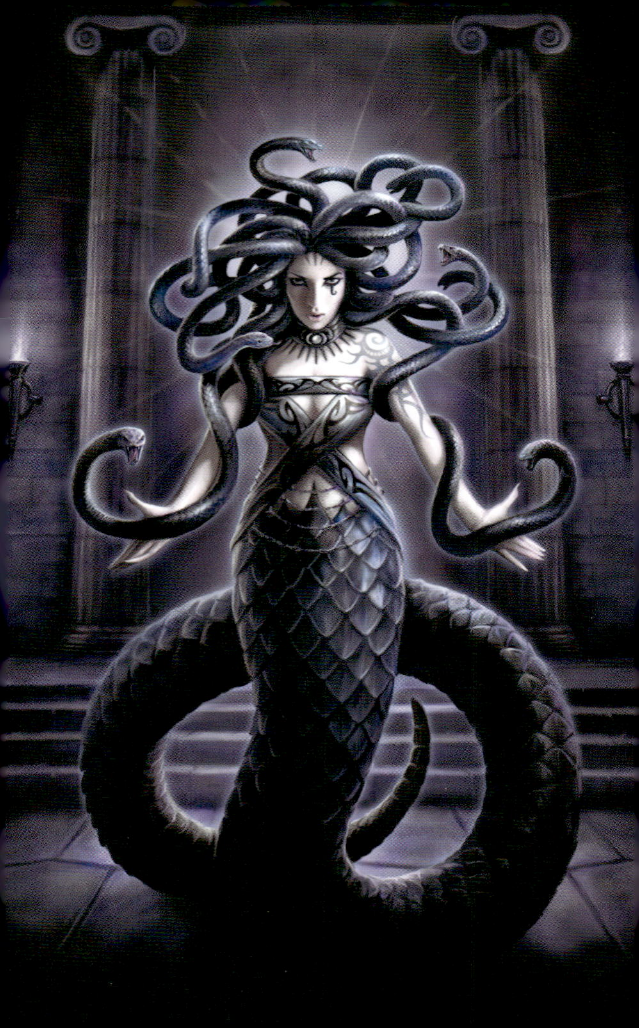

Serpent's Spell
The Shadow Self

Medusa slivers toward us. Her hair, a tangle of snakes, writhes and contorts above and around her. Her arms are outstretched, commanding respect from all who come near.

In Greek Mythology, the cursed Medusa was punished by Athena for betraying her. She was sent to a faraway island and transformed physically so that no man would ever desire her. However, this did not stop Medusa from beckoning people to look in her direction. One glance from her hypnotic eyes would turn whoever looked at her to stone.

There are many things in life that we would prefer to not acknowledge or look at closely. This slivering serpent, banished to the recesses of our own mind, represents those shadows within our self that we would prefer stay hidden.

It is important to remember that we all have a shadow self. It might manifest as jealousy, anger, laziness, or self-sabotaging beliefs that prevent you from attaining your dreams and having a healthier life. Since we can neither dismiss nor heal the dark serpent within us, it is advisable to get to know it. Facing your demons and accepting them can actually be a positive thing to do. Understanding why we become jealous or angry can uncover a path towards a more balanced way of living.

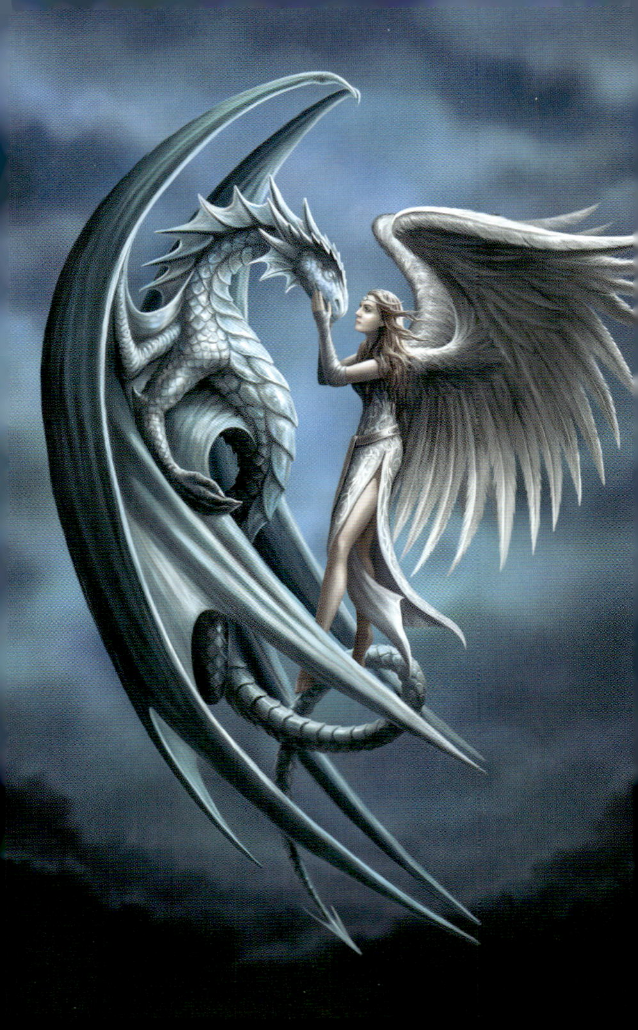

Silver Back
Respect

An angel and a dragon dance high in the night sky. As she holds his face close, the meeting of their eyes is both tender and filled with curiosity. His scales are like brushed iron, his wings like a turquoise cape. Her feathers are refined and soft; her skin, delicate and silky.

With many similarities, there are striking differences between these dance partners too. Their differences make them of interest to one another. They are both curious and respectful of what makes each of them who they are.

We will not always agree with everyone we meet. It might feel natural to push back but we are all entitled to express our opinions. Listening to others is the first step to showing respect for their beliefs.

If you have drawn this card, you might need a reminder that not everyone will see the world the same way you do. Respect is a choice and it could be important for you to take a more open-minded stance or accept that another person's view or life path is not your own. In some readings, the card will ask if it is you who is being disrespected. If you feel this to be true, it might be time to address any bias or unfair treatment.

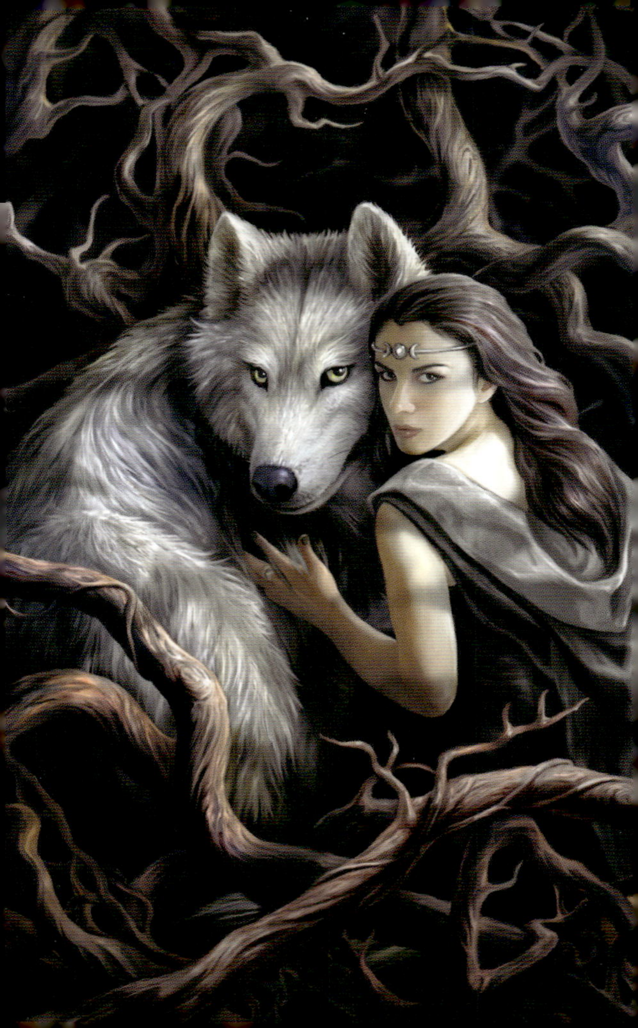

Soul Bond
Partnership

A woman and a wolf crouch within the twists and turns of tree branches. With their heads together they are one. This twosome looks in our direction, their energy, intentions, and aspirations fused by mutual respect and admiration.

While there are many things we can do by ourselves, isn't it often more satisfying when we enlist the help of someone special? This is a card of coming together with those who share a similar interest or goal.

If you have drawn this card you are being reminded of the importance of partnership and the strength of support. This could concern connecting with those who enjoy similar pastimes or, in a career-based reading, might reference the possibility or benefit of joining forces with a business or person who has similar objectives. Agreements of all kinds can be confirmed when this card is in play.

You may be used to confronting obstacles alone, but this card suggests that two heads might be better than one and that an opportunity to join with someone else is a possibility. Mergers may be on the horizon, and you may be called to share your talents and gain from the experience and skill of someone else. In a romantic reading, Soul Bond is a symbol of two hearts beating together as one, indicating that a fruitful union is in the cards.

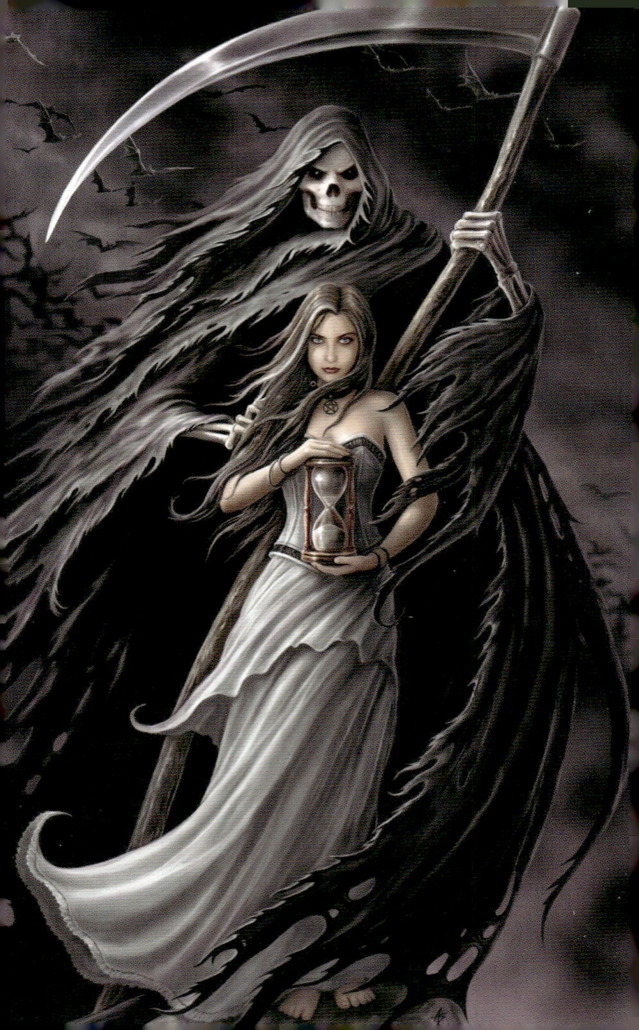

Summon the Reaper
Time

A young woman holds an hourglass between both hands, the sands of time flowing through its neck. It appears that they pass slowly but when we look away for just a moment, the vessel at the bottom appears fuller than that at the top. A reaper stands behind the woman, reminding her that everything passes eventually.

This card is less about death than life. When it makes its way into a reading, it concerns the time that is in front of us rather than what has gone. So many of us mourn the loss of youth and what we consider to be our most vibrant self, but true beauty lies within age and maturity. To be mature and experienced allows for a greater understanding of self and therefore means that we can make more informed choices for our future.

Time is always running out and there is little we can do about that. If you have drawn this card, evaluation of some kind is necessary. How will you choose to live the coming chapters of your life? What adventure is next on your list? In a general reading, you are being reminded that the sands of time wait for nobody. Maybe you need to set the wheels in motion and do something you've been itching to get on with or were putting off for a rainy day.

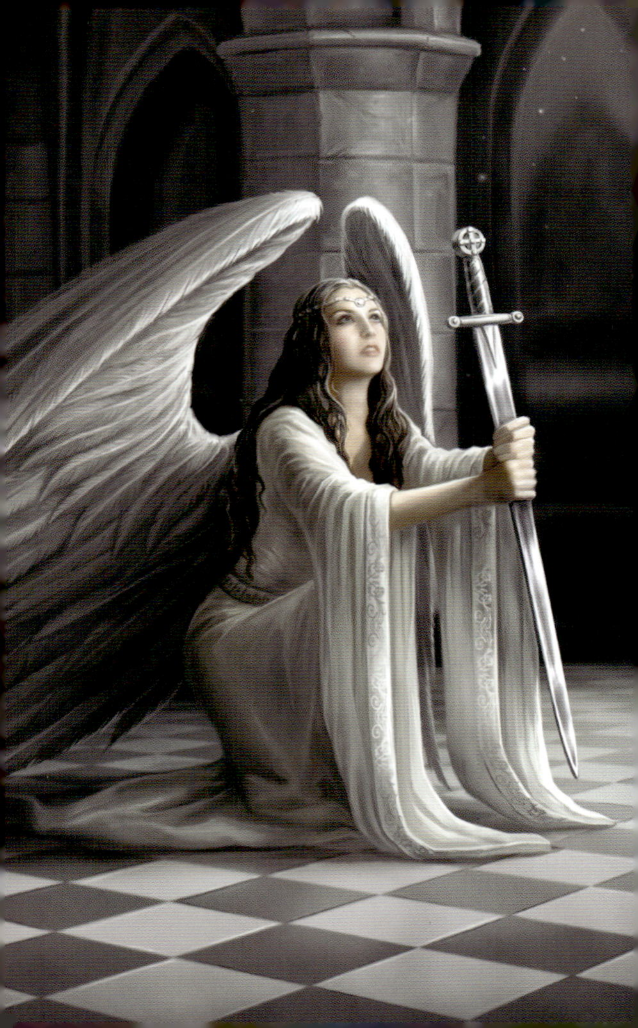

The Blessing
Signs

An angel holds her sword in front of her and prays for protection. Her gaze is strong and focused. Like a crusader, this figure seeks a blessing before going into war.

We all need, at times, some confirmation that we are on the right track: you might call it a blessing. Some of us will receive this from a trusted advisor or mature member of the family, acknowledging our path. Others will seek this out in their faith. A blessing can set us on the right track, validating a decision or dream we may be pursuing.

It is not unusual for us to receive signs from the Universe letting us know that a choice we are considering or an idea we are having is the right one. Has a song come onto the radio at just the right time, its words appropriate for something on your mind, helping you to make a decision? Has a conversation arisen with friends that perfectly aligned with a topic or idea you were thinking about? It might be that there are no coincidences, and these messages were truly meant for you. You might call them signs.

If you have drawn this card, it means that your idea is being blessed or your wishes are being answered. This is a fortuitous card, suggesting that whatever is on your mind or is the subject of your question is favored and divinely blessed.

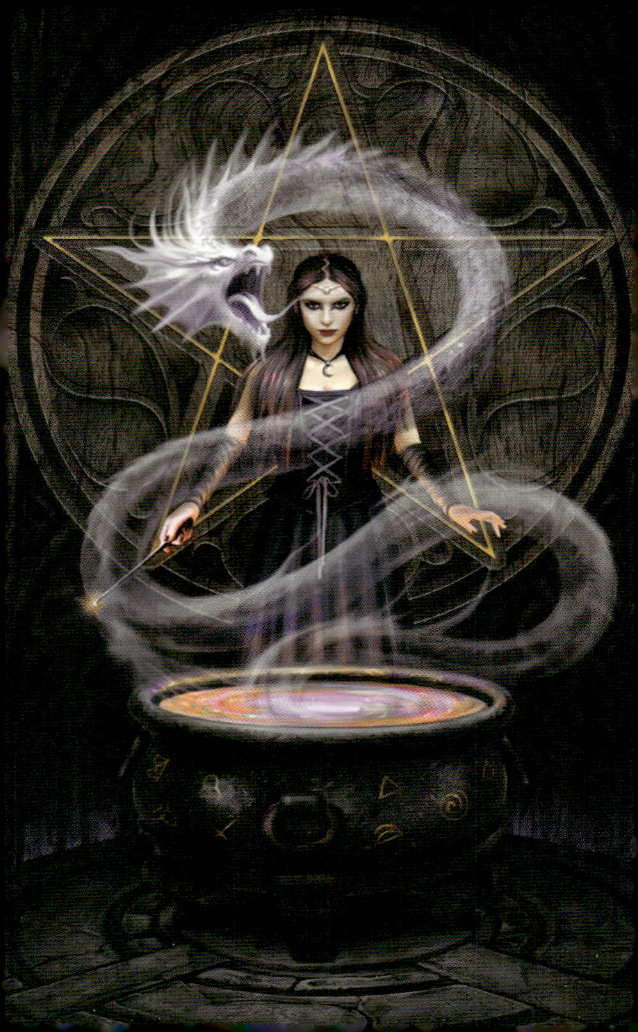

The Summoning
Creativity

A young witch stands before a cauldron. With a wave of her wand and a few powerful words, the contents begin to change color and bubble to life. From the center, a mist begins to swirl into the shape of a dragon, its mouth opening in a roar as it comes to life.

Creativity comes in many shapes and sizes. You might think, from the keyword for this card, that it concerns activities such as drawing and painting. It does, but it is also far more than that. Creativity is within us all and can manifest in a multitude of ways. Whether you are a gardener, a DIY enthusiast or someone who enjoys keeping a journal, creativity can and will arise within you whether or not you consider yourself to be creative.

This card is not only for the creative types. When this card arrives in romantic readings or acts as an answer to a problem, it is suggesting that you become inventive in your thought process. This might mean thinking outside the box and looking at a new way of doing something.

If you have drawn this card, how might you be innovative today? You might be inspired to participate in a creative project, or it might make sense for you to try a new or unconventional approach to dealing with an old problem.

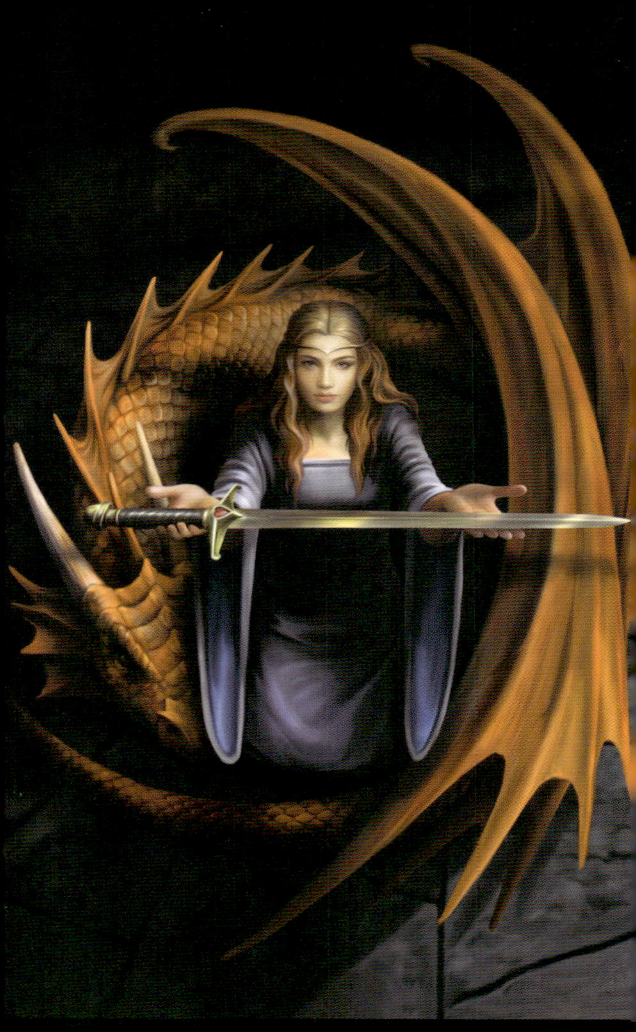

The Truth
Honesty

A woman crouches within the wings of a dragon and confidently offers you a sword. A flash of light reflects off its blade; the weapon is a symbol of the truth. Looking into your eyes, she asks that you consider what is true and what is not.

This card of honesty sometimes requires you to be honest with others, but it will always encourage you to be honest with yourself. There will be occasions when this is easier said than done. We have all experienced denial of one kind or another. The Truth card suggests that you contemplate what you truly know to be real in a situation. This can lead to inner conflict, since the truth can sometimes be ugly or hurtful, but authenticity and sincerity can only ever be the real winner.

If you have drawn this card, then you know what it is you must do. This is not a time for avoidance since fairness is paramount. In some readings, the truth will become revealed from an external source and will need to be accepted. However, in other consultations with the cards, you are being motivated to speak up about what you consider to be morally right and fair.

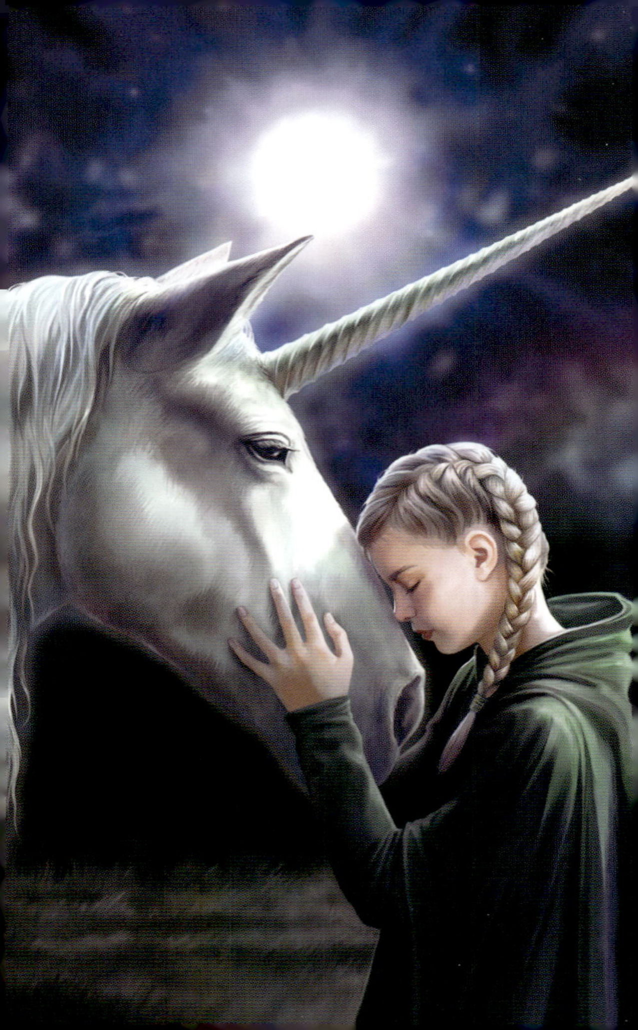

The Wish
Desire

A youngster rests her forehead on a unicorn's snout. With her eyes closed, she makes a wish under the light of the moon. Is the animal a carrier of wishes or have the two made a pact, sharing the same desire?

For some, wishes may seem fanciful but the mere act of wishing can stimulate the imagination. When we think about something we would like to happen, we naturally begin to think about ways in which it might come true. This creates a realistic bridge between what we desire and ultimately receiving it. There is a difference between productive wishing and wishful thinking.

If you have drawn this card, then your wish may soon be granted. However, it might not materialize unless your dream is coupled with action. You may desire a new living space, a better relationship or a dream job. This card could suggest that this is not as far away from reality as you might think and encourages you to carve a path towards your goal.

Of course, it is important to think about the nature of your desires. Some wishes will be more obtainable and others will have hidden costs attached to them. How would your life change for the better, or worse, if your dream actually did come true?

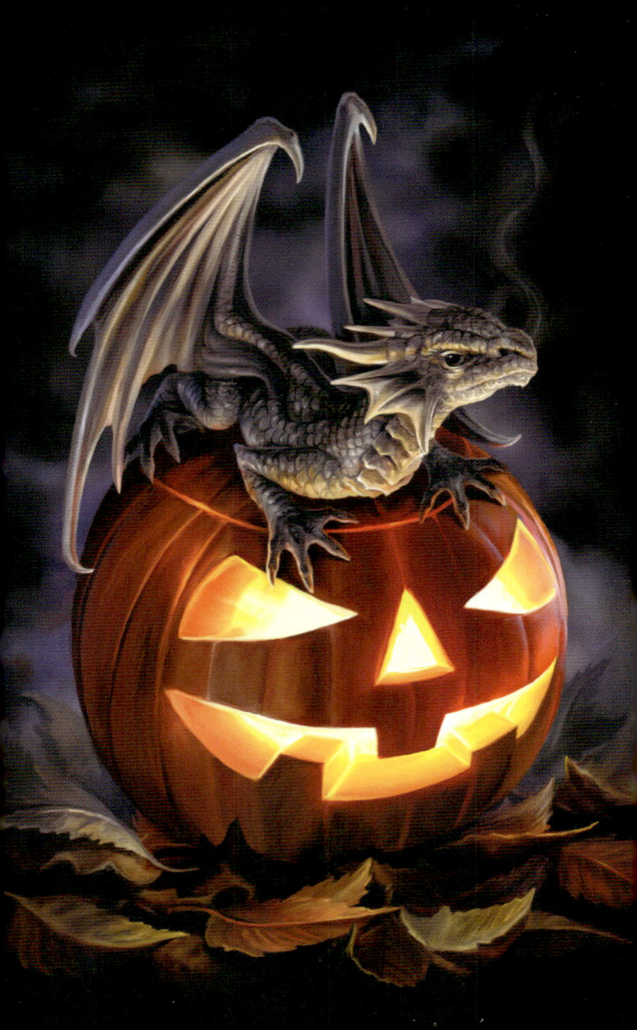

Trick or Treat
Choice

A small dragon lands upon the lid of a jack-o'-lantern. The pumpkin is lit from within, revealing a warm but slightly unsettling smile. Beneath it is a layer of autumn leaves, suggesting the darker and colder side of the year, when many choose to celebrate All Hallows' Eve.

Trick or Treating is a part of modern-day Halloween customs. Children visit the homes of neighbors, in the hope that they'll receive a handful of candy. It is less likely, these days, that they will perform a trick since many adults will stock up beforehand and enjoy participating in the celebrations.

If you receive this card, then a choice is before you. It suggests that there is more than one way to progress and that you are being given options. To be given a choice is a luxury but we must not forget that responsibility comes with the power of choosing. Consideration or advice may be needed before committing to one choice or another.

What we do in the present will have an effect on what happens at a later date. Being conscious of how your actions could influence your life and the life of others, even in the distant future, is part of this card's core message.

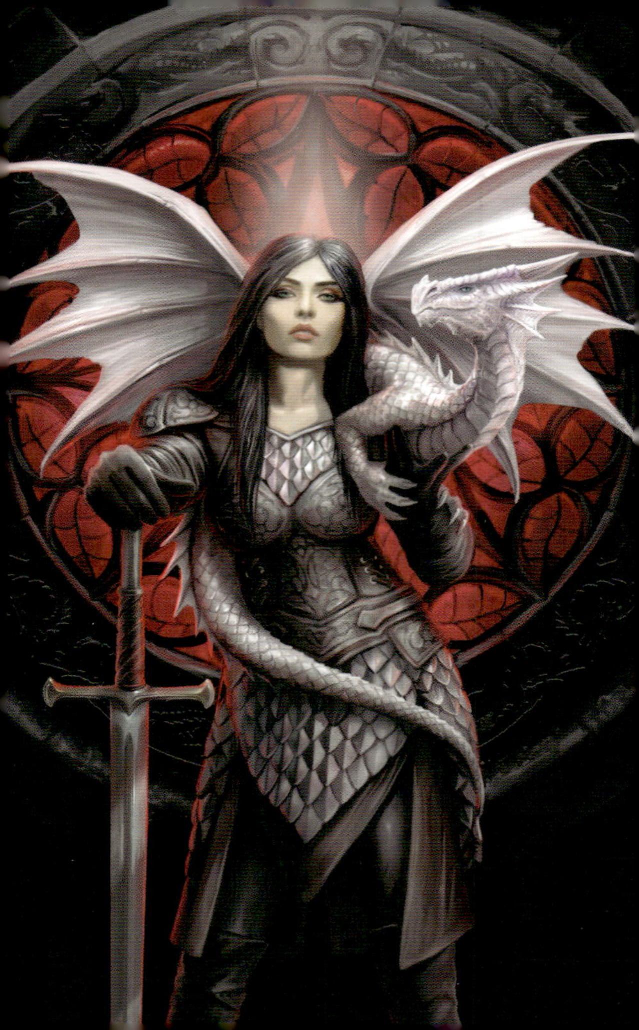

Valor
Battle

A confident woman, dressed in armor and holding onto a sword, looks piercingly into our eyes. You might think she is an angel at first but notice the icy cool dragon perched on her shoulders with his wings spread. In front of a red stained-glass window, the light reflecting on her sword resembles blood.

This card suggests that battle is necessary or inevitable. There will be circumstances when we are called into conflict and must consider the best method of response. In some situations, choosing not to respond or enter into combat is the best course of action, but this card reminds us there will be times when it is vital for you to stand your ground and fight.

The appearance of this card could signify that there is tension in the air. Quarrels and other kinds of non-physical warfare could be heading your way so donning your own armor, readying for counterattack, could be your best and only option. Unfortunately, we all fall prey to criticisms and condemnation from others. Valor reminds us that there are some disputes we simply cannot walk away from.

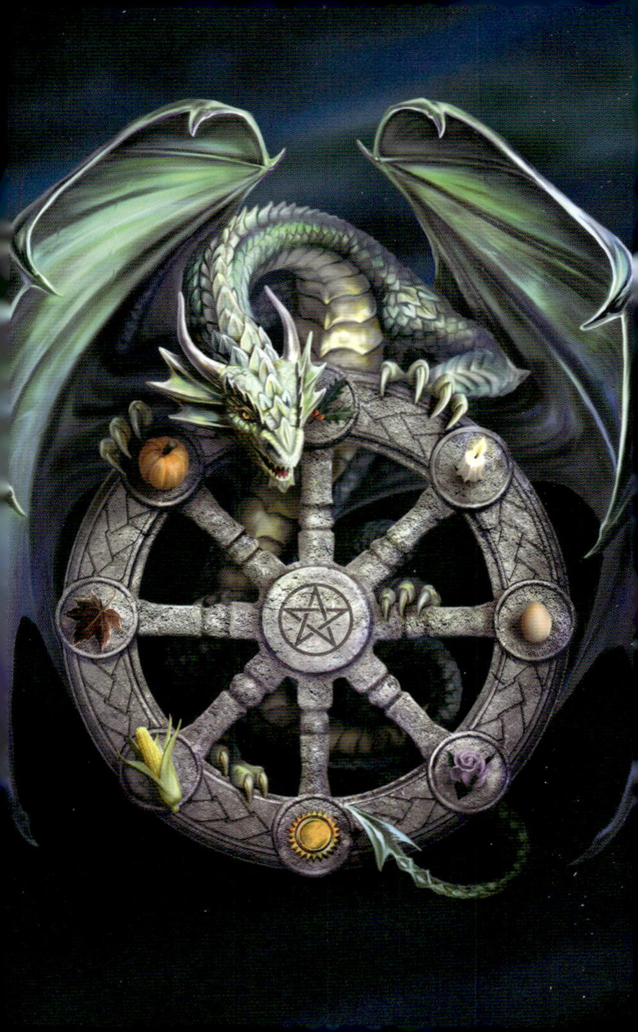

Wheel of the Year
Cycles

A fearless green dragon mounts a wheel. With her tail wrapped around its stone perimeter, it would appear that she is turning it. Eight spokes fan out from a central pentagram and at the tip of each is a symbol, representing the Sabbats. As the wheel turns, so does the year, and each of these eight holidays is commemorated. Beginning at Samhain (the pumpkin), nature buds and sheds its leaves through Yule, Imbolc, Ostara, Beltane, Litha, Lughnasadh and Mabon.

The Wheel of the Year is a card of cycles. Throughout the seasons, things sprout, grow, and then wither and die. This is a fact of life and we must allow it to flow naturally without resistance or interruption.

If you have drawn this card, you are being reminded that life is all about change. There are often many changes in life that we are incapable of preventing. Not all of these will be life altering and while some will be feared, others will be welcomed.

This large dragon confirms that change is taking effect and reminds you that sometimes the best course of action is to go with the flow. The wise person will recognize when participation is pointless and it is best to stand back and not react. Now is a time to yield and understand that the Universe has a greater plan, even if it is not what you had expected!

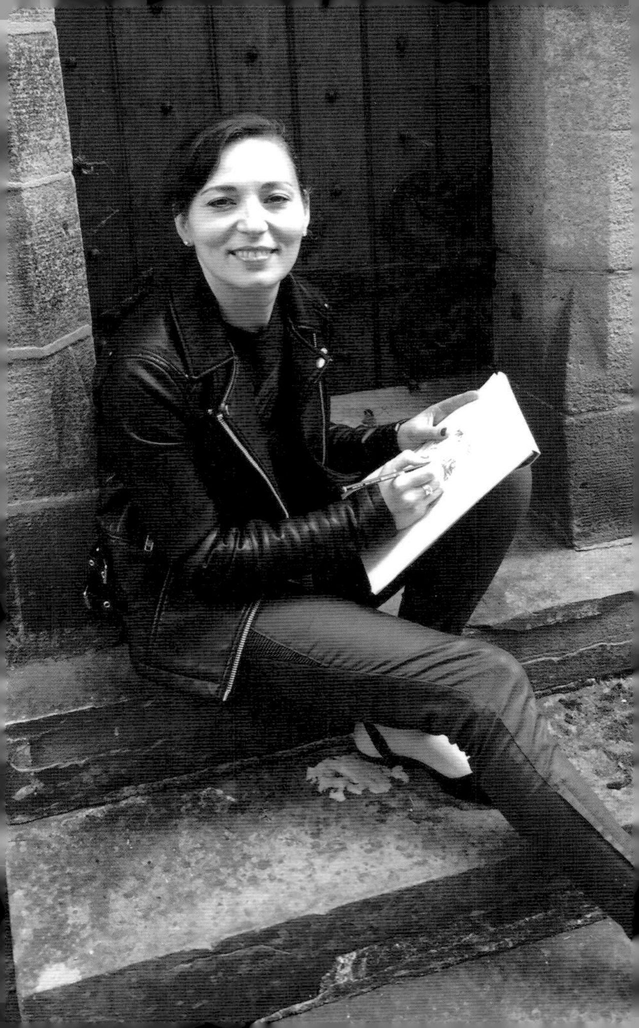

About the Artist

The fantasy art of Anne Stokes has been featured on many book covers, games and merchandise products. Her striking designs and lifelike portrayals of fantasy subjects are widely acclaimed. Anne's fantasy artworks encompass a broad range of subjects, from romantic and magical enchanted forests, to the dark underworld of Gothic vampires, with many portraits of her favorite subject, the dragon.

Anne's art has travelled the world, attracting fans who love fantasy and her unique and eye-catching interpretations of classic subjects. She posts regularly on social media and makes videos discussing her art. You can follow her on Facebook, Instagram and YouTube, all of which can be found at **@AnneStokesArt** and her website **www.annestokes.com** where there is also further information and a gallery of some of Anne's art.

Anne lives and works in Yorkshire in the UK with her partner John Woodward, son Leo and their three dogs.

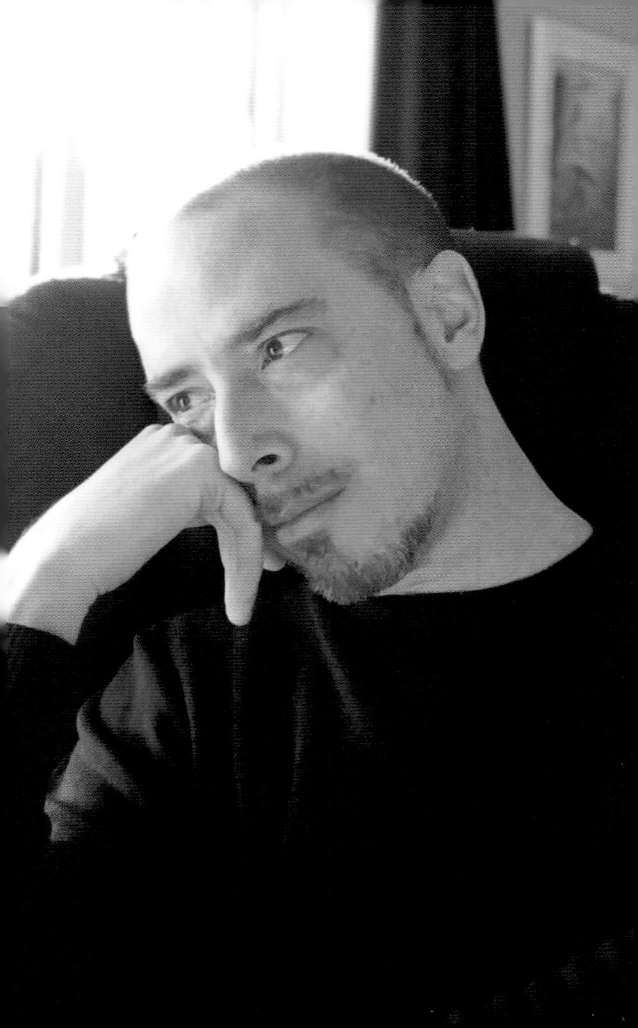

About the Author

Steven Bright was born in London in 1972. He began his card reading journey in 1996 and has read for many clients throughout the world. He is the author of *Tarot: Your Personal Guide* and *The Oracle Creator: The Modern Guide to Creating a Tarot or Oracle Deck*. He has created two divination decks, *Spirit Within Tarot* and *Rainbow Kipper*. He contributed cards to *Pride Tarot: A Collaborative Deck*, published by U.S. Games Systems, Inc. As well as reading cards, Steven has taught public classes and workshops, including presenting at the UK Tarot Conference, at the Tarot of the British Isles Conference and at the London Tarot Festival. Steven is the co-founder and co-editor of *The Esotoracle*, a magazine focused on all methods of divination.

Instagram: @stevenbrightuk

Notes

Notes

For our complete line of tarot decks, books, meditation cards, oracle sets, and other inspirational products please visit our website:
www.usgamesinc.com

Follow us:

Published by
U.S. GAMES SYSTEMS, INC.
179 Ludlow Street
Stamford, CT 06902 USA
www.usgamesinc.com